January
....the beginning

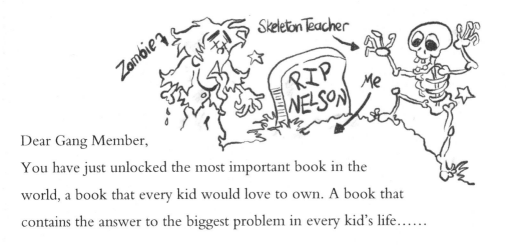

Dear Gang Member,

You have just unlocked the most important book in the world, a book that every kid would love to own. A book that contains the answer to the biggest problem in every kid's life……

How To Not Get Grounded…..Ever!

Bringing you this information has been no easy task. Many have fallen along the way. As you can see, I myself have paid the ultimate price. I was hunted by swarms of teachers, tracked by gangs of angry parents, and tortured by hordes of school janitors. All of them failed to stop me. And now this book is safe in your hands. I only hope that my death was worth it. Read on…and remember….trust no-one.

Signed -Nelson *(Ex-kid + Grounded Gang President)*

P.S. This book has a secret built-in scanner. While you were reading this it tested you to see if you are worthy of this knowledge. If you are not, it will self-destruct in 10 seconds. I recommend you run!

Congratulations! I see you passed the first test!

What's that?

How am I writing this book if I'm dead?

Alright, so I'm not dead!

One of my teachers wished I was dead once. I heard him mumble it under his breath while he was marking my math homework. The dog had eaten it the night before but luckily he had thrown it back up. It was still a little bit wet when I handed it in, and it smelled really bad, and I only got a C-…………………….but at least I didn't get detention!

Anyway, it is true that a lot of grown-ups would do anything to keep you from learning the secrets in this book.

So, read on.

But remember, THEY ARE ALWAYS WATCHING YOU!

Really Nelson????
You think anyone cares about your stupid little book? - Mildred

Look Mildred, I was trying to be scary! Anyway, why are you writing in my private book? You're my little sister and you have to do what I say.
SO STOP OR I'M TELLING MOM! -Nelson

Stuff to Learn

Don't you think you're being just a little over dramatic? -Mildred

That's it! I'm telling Mom! -Nelson

Remember, this is the most important book ever! Adults everywhere would just love to get their hands on it. That is why we have to keep it hidden.

On the next page you will find a fake cover. If you are reading this in a public put the fake cover on the front of the book to make adults think you are reading something else. Don't worry, it's not anything stupid. In fact, it's just the sort of thing adults want you to read; something that they think is cool. Do not use the fake cover trick too often though. It may lead to lots of questions about what you are learning, and that would be bad, trust me! If they start snooping just tell them your tummy hurts and that you need to go to the bathroom.

That always scares them.*

Yeah? Then you would have to show her this book, stupid! -Mildred

---

* This may backfire with Moms. They are obsessed with what you do in the bathroom. I once caught mine taking a photo of my poop to show the doctor. That taught me not to forget to flush, I can tell you! – Nelson

How to get A's and win medals

while writing poems about your feelings and getting paid lots of money

by Mitch.E Butt

More Stuff To Learn

Well, now that we can talk safely, let's begin. In the next few pages you will learn all the stuff you need to know to be in the Grounded Gang. Obviously, the big problem with the Grounded Gang is that we all keep getting grounded! This makes it very difficult to have meetings. That's why we have the book. I put everything we need to know in these pages. Then if you can't make it to a meeting you can catch up later.

Like this! -Nelson

You will also notice that I sometimes add extra notes. These will make sure we always have the latest information on how to avoid getting grounded. All members are encouraged to add their own notes. IMPORTANT: Allowing anyone NOT in the gang to write in it, especially girls, is strictly against the rules!

I'm not in your gang AND I'm a girl so I win already! - Mildred

We hold meetings every month at our top secret base. All the stuff we talk about at meetings is top secret. The only place it's allowed to go is in this book. If you're grounded and can't make it to a meeting you must send a letter explaining why you aren't there. Then, when you are no longer grounded, you can read the book to see what you missed. The book never, ever leaves the base!!!!!!!!!

GET OUT OF MY BOOK! -NELSON

The Grounded Gang Rules

1. You do not talk about the Grounded Gang.
2. No, really. Do not talk about the Grounded Gang.
3. Especially to adults. They are the reason we are all in the Grounded Gang and are NOT to be trusted.
4. No talking about girls either! It's bad enough that my sister is one of them and I have to live in the same house as her.
5. Never let anyone follow you to our secret hide-out, especially our enemies!
6. Learn who our enemies are.
7. Shirt and shoes are optional at meetings…unless your feet smell bad. Then you have to hang them out the window.
8. Anyone grounded for longer than eight weeks may ask to be rescued.
9. If you are in the Gang you have to help with all rescues.
10. Yes, you do.
11. Even if it's cold out.
12. And dark.
13. Look, we all have to go, ALRIGHT!

Right, now I am telling Mom! -Mildred

You do that and maybe I'll tell Mom how her best bowl REALLY got broken last week! -Nelson

More Grounded Gang Rules

14. If you are grounded and aren't able to come to a meeting, you must submit the reason in writing.
15. All reasons will be judged by the group and scored on the unfair-o'meter below.

16. If you score a 4 or above we will form an escape committee to free you.
17. Anytime someone says the word 'what?' you are officially allowed to call them a chicken butt.
18. Each member is allowed one fart per meeting. Anybody farting more than once will have to go outside until it's all out of them.★
19. This writing is really small so you'll have trouble reading it and say 'what?'
20. Chicken butt.

★In special situations air freshener may be allowed instead. Like the time Jim ate a pile of dead beetles for a dare and couldn't stop his butt 'talking' for the rest of the week.

Stuff You MUST Be Able To Say 'Yes' To, If You Want To Be One Of Us

1. Are you a boy?
2. Do you get grounded at least once a month?
3. Are you usually grounded for things that are not your fault?
4. When you are grounded, should your Mom and Dad really have just been a little bit more understanding?
5. ......especially since you had a good excuse?
6. Do teachers only say your name when they want to kill you?
7. Are boys better than girls?
8. Are you good at keeping secrets?
9. Can you burp on demand?
10. Are you hard to scare?.....BEHIND YOU!.....That was a test.
11. Did you pass the test?
12. Are you sure you passed the test?
13. Can you make a word using these four letters? W H A T
14. Are you a chicken butt?

15. Did Nelson's little sister ever catch him watching her movie about the Princess and the butterfly? A movie he said only dumb girls would watch. And was he crying at the bit where he thought the butterfly was dead? -Mildred

16. Do you wish you never had a little sister? -Nelson

Some More Rules

Members of the gang must greet each other with the secret handshake before every meeting.*

1. Greet it.
2. Grip it.
3. Pick it.
4. Mash it.
5. Eat it.

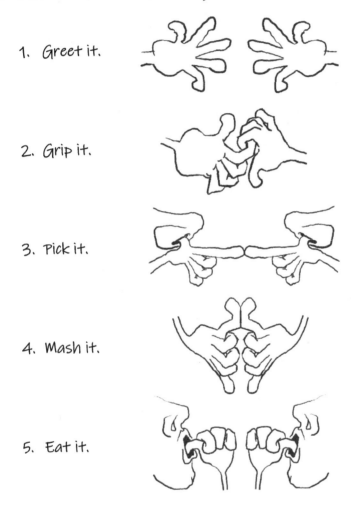

*If you have recently been ill you MUST inform the Gang before doing this. We do not want a repeat of last spring when Tommy failed to tell us he was recovering from a case of bad diarrhea and we all got so ill that some of us thought we would have to wear a diaper. -Nelson

Grounded Gang Dress Code

All Grounded Gang members are expected NOT to dress nicely at every meeting. Anyone dressed like they are going to visit their Grandparents will be asked to leave immediately.

Level 1: T-shirts

Acceptable Pics — Skulls, Ninjas, Dragons

Unacceptable Pics — Princesses, Bunnies, Moms

Level 2: Pants

Acceptable — Anything comfortable

Unacceptable — No pants

Level 3: Footwear

Acceptable — Anything that doesn't smell bad

Unacceptable — What did you step in?

Grounded Gang Secret Codes

Because you never know who's listening!

Right, time to learn about…

OUR ENEMIES!

Study these pages carefully. Not long ago these were just regular people. The only thing wrong with them was that they **<u>chose</u>** to spend their days at school, without being given a wedgie, or threatened with no TV, or anything!

Now it seems as though their only purpose in life is to see us grounded for as long as possible. I don't know what made them change but until we find out, all we can do is be really, really careful.

Take time to learn who they are. Then, the next time they attack, just maybe we'll be ready.

But never, ever, ever trust them.

That's just crazy! -Mildred

The Hammer

Name: Mr. Mallet

Job: School Principal

Nickname: The Hammer

Weaknesses: Unknown

Strengths: Scary voice. Scary office. Scary eyes. Parents love him.

Weapon of Choice: Making kids learn stuff.

The Law

Name: Mrs. D. Tension

Job: Our teacher

Nickname: The Law

Weaknesses: Big Butt (easy for kids to hide behind)

Strengths: Hates Children

Weapon of Choice: Homework

Needles

Name: Nurse Payne

Job: School Nurse

Nickname: Needles

Weaknesses: Junk food. Sight of blood. Doesn't like sick kids.

Strengths: Immune to all germs.

Weapon of Choice: Medication and extra sticky band aides.

The Mop

Name: Mr. McTavy

Job: School Janitor

Nickname: The Mop

Weaknesses: Doesn't like to do any work.

Strengths: Is allowed to carry sharp objects on school grounds.

Weapon of Choice: Bleach and cleaning the drinking fountain with his old socks.

Gas

Name: Mildred Mulberry

Job: Head Lunch Lady

Nickname: Gas (She burns everything…and her cooking smells like farts.)

Weaknesses: Food gets stuck in her moustache.

Strengths: Gets paid to make kids feel ill every day.

Weapon of Choice: Meatloaf

The Rattle

Name: Mr. Bulk

Job: Gym Teacher

Nickname: The Rattle (has a brain the size of a pea).

Weaknesses: Counting and Reading

Strengths: Is allowed to cause kids pain and call it "exercise".

Weapon of Choice: Sports

D.I.E.

Name: The Hert Sisters

Job: Students....and making our lives miserable.

Nickname: D.I.E. (Danni, Isabella, Emily).

Weaknesses: Unknown

Strengths: They are not human.

Weapon of Choice: Hating everyone in the Grounded Gang.

Map to Our Secret Base

(So you know where to meet!)

> # TOP SECRET
> # DO NOT LOOK UNDER
> # HERE UNLESS YOU ARE
> # IN THE GROUNDED GANG
> -Nelson

Why won't this peel back? -Mildred

Are you crazy enough to think I'd leave a real map in here? No way! I can't risk the base being discovered! -Nelson

Tell me where it is or I'll tell everyone at school you wear pink underpants!
-Mildred

For the last time. Mom accidentally washed them with my red socks! Now go away already! -Nelson

Sure thing, girly pants! -Mildred

The Grounded Gangs Pledge of Allegiance

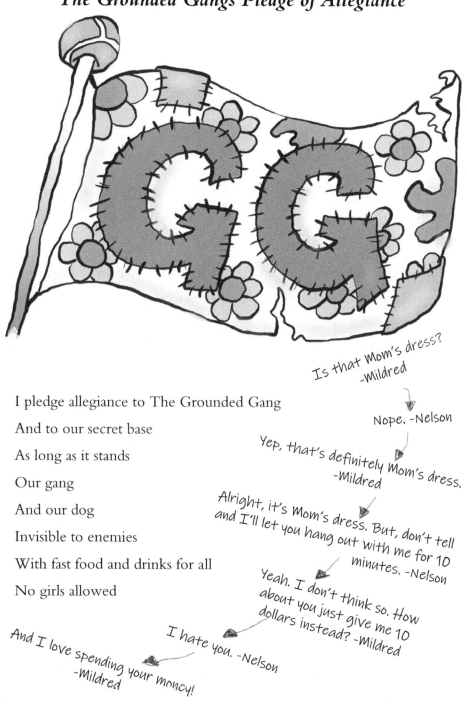

I pledge allegiance to The Grounded Gang

And to our secret base

As long as it stands

Our gang

And our dog

Invisible to enemies

With fast food and drinks for all

No girls allowed

Is that Mom's dress? -Mildred

Nope. -Nelson

Yep, that's definitely Mom's dress. -Mildred

Alright, it's Mom's dress. But, don't tell and I'll let you hang out with me for 10 minutes. -Nelson

Yeah. I don't think so. How about you just give me 10 dollars instead? -Mildred

I hate you. -Nelson

And I love spending your money! -Mildred

Final Thoughts

And flush it down the toilet. -Mildred

Well that's it Gang. All you need to know. I hope that you'll treat this information with the respect it deserves.

All that's left to say is how proud I am to be your leader and I promise that I will do everything in my power to keep us safe from all those trying to ground us.

Maybe one day, one sweet day, we'll be able to put all of this behind us and change the name of our Gang to something that will reflect the better days ahead. A really cool name like……

The cool kids who could all have girlfriends if they wanted but don't because girls will always be a waste of time, even if my Dad says that one day I'll change my mind about that……Gang.

(The CKWCAHGITWBDBGWABAWOTEIMDSTODICMMATG for short)

Okay, it needs some work. But trust me, one day getting grounded will just be a bad memory…..and we shall be free……to leave our bedrooms whenever we want!

See you next month. -Nelson

Trust me Nelson. No girl will ever want to be your girlfriend. -Mildred

That's okay Mildred. I forgive you. And I love you. -Nelson

What? -Mildred

CHICKENBUTT! -Nelson

Extra Bit That Can't Wait

You are not going to believe what I just found out!
This is the big one guys! This explains it all. Now I think I know why we keep getting grounded! Cant talk now. Someone's coming. I'll fill you in next time I see you.

~~February~~

~~March~~

~~April~~

~~May~~

~~June~~

~~July~~

August

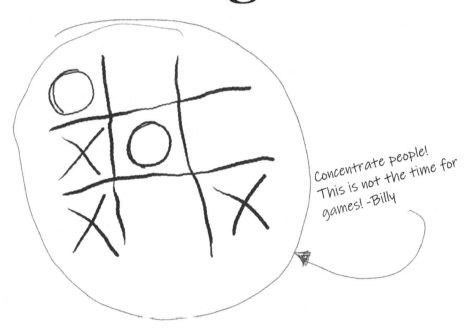

Concentrate people! This is not the time for games! -Billy

Emergency Meeting of the Ground Gang

Dear Gang Member,

So, it has been a long time since our last meeting. But with all the problems we've faced lately it's been really difficult.

Problem #1 -Nelson Got Grounded. No one knows why but none of us has seen him since the last time he wrote in this book. I went to his house and asked his Mom where he was but she said that he was grounded…for life! Our friend….our leader….gone….and it's kind of hard to have a gang with no gang president. Oh yeah, his little sister is grounded too. Well, we think she was grounded. No-one has seen her either. No big loss.

Problem #1 -School Got Crazy. It's become like everything we do gets us in trouble! We used to be the best kids there….okay, maybe not the best kids, but we weren't that bad! Now it's like the staff love the bad kids and hate the good kids (that's us)!

Problem #3 -All Of Our Enemies Became Friends With Our Parents. It was bad enough seeing them everyday at school but suddenly they're everywhere. I came home one day to find The Hammer sitting in the kitchen laughing with my Dad! That's right, the Hammer was laughing! I didn't even know he knew what laughing was! To make it even worse, the teachers have started 'advising' our parents on how to punish us! It's crazy, and a miracle, that we survived to see summer vacation!

MORE! Get to the next page already! -Billy

But, that was two long months ago. Two happy months were spent hanging out at the base with no enemies to bother us. But, next week that ends and we have to go back to school….for a whole year!

That is why the Grounded Gang has to, officially, start meeting again! We can't wait any longer for Nelson to be released. Unless we stay together, we will never survive middle school. We'll end up grounded for life….or worse! Staying together is our only hope!

And the first thing we will need is a new leader. Hopefully it won't be for long….just until Nelson is finally free. Until then, we have to meet tomorrow and vote on who is going to be in charge.

Tomorrow. After breakfast. DON'T BE LATE!

Signed, Billy

What about being buried alive? Isn't that worse? -Brain

Or being eaten alive by cats? -Rock

That's stupid! Why would a cat eat you? -Brain

They do! I saw it in a movie once. This man was trapped in a sewer and all these cats came out of the dark and started biting him -Rock

Sewer? They were rats not cats! -Brain

So, my sisters kitten isn't trying to kill me? -Rock

You're a moron! -Brain

Next Day

A letter from the new President of the Grounded Gang.

So, that was a bad idea!

No-one wanted to be leader, I get it. But voting while I was stuck on the toilet looking for toilet paper really wasn't fair. Even less fair was how you wrote your votes on toilet paper! If I didn't know better I might think that you stole the toilet paper on purpose! Well, I guess I don't have a choice now, do I! I'm the new President of the Grounded Gang, thanks a lot! I don't know why I trusted you all!

We've ONLY been friends since kindergarten…I should know better! So, as President, my first official decision will be to make a rule that, from now on, the clubhouse always has enough toilet paper. Gutsy, that's your job….try not to eat any of it! My second job will be to find out why we keep getting grounded! My third job is to discover why our parents do everything that the teachers tell them to! It's just not right! My fourth job will be to hire someone to keep the secret base tidy. Maybe we can train a monkey to come in once a week to make it look nice? We can even have a girl do it if we have to! SiFi, look into that for me, I mean us.

How will it be a secret base if we have girls who know where it is? -SiFi

My final job will be to work out a way to free Nelson. I mean we don't even know why he's been grounded. It's not like him to get in trouble….. Something strange is going on and I plan to find out what! And when I say 'I', I mean us. Hey, I think I'm starting to get the hang of this being in charge thing! Okay Grounded Gang, let's have a good meeting. We will officially meet here again next month. Make sure you put your new membership cards in the book this week and definitely check out the list of stuff you need to do. And remember, as long as we are at the clubhouse we are safe. But when you leave here, be careful….trust no-one….try to keep the place clean….and if you use the last of the toilet paper make sure you get a new roll.

Later, -Billy

What about that time he put that nest of bees in his sister's bedroom? -Rock

Or the time he glued his sister's hair to her pillow while she was asleep? -SiFi

And what about the time he tried to sell his sister's hamster by pretending it was a really small dog? -Brain

OKAY, WE GET IT!!!! He doesn't get along with his sister! Other than all the stuff he does to her, it's not like him to get in trouble! -Billy

Grounded Gang Members

Right then, put your membership cards in here for safekeeping. It's way too dangerous for us to be carrying them on us right now. If anyone asks you about the Grounded Gang tell them that it doesn't exist anymore. We can't risk what happened to Nelson happening to us. In fact, just tell everyone that we started a band instead. Oh, and that I'm the lead singer. The best looking one is always the leader singer. *Ha, ha.....oh wait...Is he serious? -Rock*

Oh, and remember to update your secret scratch and sniff smell. If you are ever taken prisoner it's our only way to know if you are really you and not some sort of imposter/zombie pretending to be you. Oh, everyone is not allowed to use 'butt' as their secret smell. That just makes it confusing. And as I'm the one who has to test the smells, it also makes it totally disgusting.

If you want to make a few notes about each other please be nice. We've all been best friends for a really long time so I think we can all agree to stop bringing up stories from our past. Especially the one about a certain gang member who was really, really young and didn't know that dressing as a ninja with a pink tutu on the first day of kindergarten wasn't quite as cool as he thought it was.

He's talking about himself isn't he? -Gutsy

Yep, I'll show you the photo later, it's hilarious! -SiFi

Oh, one more thing. Membership fees are also due so empty out your pockets and leave $10 on this page ……....do not forget! We've been getting through a lot of soda lately and need to buy more. Free soda isn't free you know!?

THAT'S IT?! 2 coins for Cheesy Clown, 2 useless notes, a pencil, a toy soldier's arm, half a candy bar and a dead spider! We are officially broke! -Billy

Nelson

Age: 11

Longest Grounding: Jan – Present (new record)!

Unknown

I had to do Nelsons for him. I couldn't find a recent photo but I found one from when he was three....and updated it! This is what I think he looks like now -Billy

Why has he got a beard? He's only 11! -SiFi

Alright! So I can't draw! -Billy

He looks older than my Dad! -Brain

Billy

Age: 11

Longest Grounding: 12½ days (released ½ day early for good behavior).

GROUNDED GANG MEMBER
Name: Billy Gruff
Codename: The Goat
Skills: Video Games
 + Worlds Best Sniper
 (in video games)
Secret Smell: 〰〰〰

No Fear -Billy

That's not fair! That's not a real smell! If he's allowed to use that then I'm allowed to use my butt! -Rock

Why are you so desperate to use your butt as your secret smell??? -Gutsy

I didn't wash it for 10 days especially....it smells so bad right now! My neighbors dog sniffed it yesterday and ran away from home. -Rock

New item for the next meeting. How to get ~~new~~ ~~better~~ ~~some~~ ANY new members. -Billy

Brain

Age: 11

Longest Grounding: 2 weeks + an extra week to clean up the mess he made in his laboratory/bedroom during those 2 weeks.

My secret smell is a mixture of the following chemicals....
Beao
Uragirl
Taninoil
Tenizracket
I call it BUTT for short! -Brain

Oh, ha ha! Very funny! -Billy

That's a lie! No-one can speak girl! -Brain

Si Fi

Age: 11

Longest Grounding: 6 weeks

For showing that aliens are real! -Si Fi

GROUNDED GANG MEMBER

Name: Simon Figgs

Codename: Si Fi

Skills: Speaks English, Alien & Girl

Secret Smell:

I chose to write my secret smell in alien language. -Si Fi

BUTT -Si Fi

Errrr....that's not exactly true is it? -DD

Okay! Aliens are not real and writing words upside down do not make them alien language! Oh, and that smell is disgusting! -Billy

Town Hall Satellite Dish Destroyed by Boy Looking for Aliens

Double Dare

Age: 11

Longest Grounding: 4 weeks

I broke both my legs jumping off a roof for a bet. Totally worth it! -DD

GROUNDED GANG MEMBER

Name: Chris P. Bacon
Codename: Double Dare
Skills: Eating strangers boogers
Secret Smell:

Seriously, is there anything he won't do for a bet? -Si Fi

You mean like change his name? -Gutsy

Or eat a strangers boogers? -Brain

Or eat a spider while cutting his own hair? -Rock

Nope! I've done all of those. I win! -DD

Yeah!....You win!!!! -DD

Flowers, perfume and smelly candles....just kidding, its butt! -DD

Your name is Norice Roberts. It doesn't mean just write any name! -Brain

The Rock

Age: 11

???????? -Brain

Longest Grounding: 10 days minus 1 day for good behavior =8 -Rock

GROUNDED GANG MEMBER

Name: Abe Lincoln

Codename: The Rock

Skills: I forgot. Wait, no, it's gone again. I forgot. Oh yeah, that's it. My skill is remembering stuff.

Secret Smell:

Why is he called The Rock? -Si Fi

It's because I'm big and have lots of muscles -Rock

Actually Rock, it's because on your last three report cards your teachers all wrote that you were as clever as a Rock! -Gutsy

Oh, is that why? I thought they'd written I was as clever as a <u>sock</u>. A rock is way better. -Rock

Sssssshhhhh.......It's a secret......BUTT I promise to tell you after you smell it! -Rock

Oh, good grief! -Billy

41

Gutsy

Age: 11

Longest Grounding: 2 weeks

With no dessert! It was pure torture!
   -Gutsy

GROUNDED GANG MEMBER

Name: Gregory Black

Codename: Gutsy

Skills: Eating...mostly food. Occasionally a toenail. I'm not picky.

Secret Call:

Did you eat your membership card? -Billy

Just a few bites. I was so hungry....I couldn't help it! Gutsy

Is there anything you won't eat? -Billy

I put ketchup on it first! -Gutsy

Oh, that makes it so much better! -Billy

Buttons, butterflies, butterscotch, buttermilk. I can't think of anymore but it doesn't matter, you know where I'm going with this!
   -Gutsy

Drool

Age: 8  All of them very annoying! -Billy

Longest Grounding: 0 days.

GROUNDED GANG MEMBER

Name: Brady Gruff

Codename: Drool

Skills: Kung-Fu, Karate, Ninja skills....I've seen cartoons about all of these.

Secret Smell: 〰〰〰

Bellybutton fluff. -Drool

Well at least it's better than all the others! -Billy

Just kidding. ~~Bellybutton fluff.~~ -Drool

HEY! I'm your big brother and you have to respect me! Remember you are only in this gang because Mom and Dad say I have to take care of you! -Billy

HEY! I'm your big brother and you have to respect me! Remember you are only in this gang because Mom and Dad say I have to take care of you! -Drool

STOP COPYING ME! -Billy

STOP COPYING ME! -Drool

Chicken Butt

Age: 4. (Dog years 76. Smell years 210)   **NEW MEMBER!**

Longest Grounding: He doesn't move. So, like, forever?

GROUNDED GANG MEMBER

Name: Chickenbutt

Codename: Chickenbutt

Skills: Sleeping...Oh, and he has 3 legs, an eyepatch, and a fork for an ear.

Secret Smell:

Butt...and it's not a secret....he smells really bad! -Billy

We have a dog as a member now? And are you sure it's a dog? -Brain

All the best gangs have mascots! Plus the man in the store actually gave me money to take him! -Billy

Anyone else notice the smell in here? -DD

That, gentlemen, is the smell of success! -Billy

Nope! I think your mascot keeps farting! -Billy

My eyes are on fire! -DD

I asked him how old he was and he held up his fingers...he only has 9 and a ½ fingers!
-Billy

Mouse
Age: 9 ½
Longest Grounding: "Thank-you. Is very nice."

NEW MEMBER!

GROUNDED GANG MEMBER

Name: Stenyabulmieona Smith

Codename: Mouse

Skills: Master of escape.
Master of fitting into small spaces.
Master of being made to say things he does not understand.

Secret Smell:

Who is this? -Brain

Unknown. It smells bad though. When I asked him what it was he just pointed at the back of his pants....Hey! Wait a minute! -Billy

He's a foreign exchange student staying at my house. He speaks like no English. He's only been here 3 weeks and he's been grounded twice. I think he needs us! -Si Fi

I, Mouse. Thanking yous for me beings in yous gong. -Mouse

45

Final Thoughts

Okay guys, the Grounded Gang is officially re-united! School begins tomorrow so it's time to get ready for war! All of your assignments are posted on the next page. And before you ask………

YES. You do have to do the one you've been given!

NO. You can't swop or get extra time if you forget to do it!
We'll meet back here next month. Until then, remember, we're a gang! And that makes us like family. So watch out for eachother!

Yes Mom! -Si Fi

Assignments for Next Month

Project Free Nelson: DD + Rock.
Try to find out something new about why Nelson's been grounded. Get close to his house. See what he's up to. Oh, and while you're there try to steal some of his Mom's homemade cookies. They're good!

Get Drinks + Snacks: Gutsy. You were born for this job!

Give Chickenbutt a bath: Drool.

Protect the Base: Chickenbutt. Show us that you are more than just a mascot! And don't poop indoors....again!

The Rest: Brain, Mouse and Si Fi, we need an update on the D.I.E. Sisters. What are they doing? What are they thinking? How can we stop them from doing and thinking?

GROUNDED GANG OUT! No way! Nelsons Mom is crazy! She'll kill us if she catches us! -DD

Dare you! -Billy

I'll do it! -DD

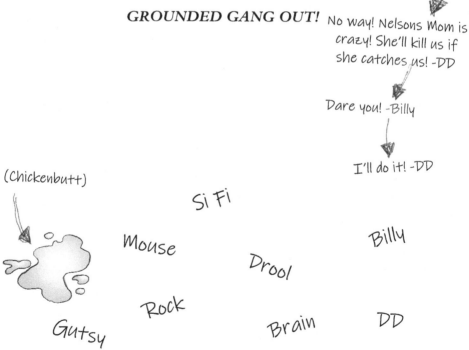

September

Okay, now that really is disgusting! Who left this here? -Billy

September Meeting

A letter from the President of The Grounded Gang.

> That's probably me. I ate a box of raw eggs and they want out! -Gutsy

Well, that month was pretty lousy! I thought the enemies would be ready to get us once we went back to school but I never saw this coming! Three of us grounded, two just released and now one of us just did a fart so bad that I can hardly breathe. And, to top it all, part of the roof fell off our top-secret base. Now, when you sit on the couch after it rains, it feels like someone just peed on it.

It's been a bad month guys. A bad, bad month. Something's not right. I can't quite put my finger on it but none of this seems to make sense. Why does everyone hate us so much? We have to find out....before it's too late! Let's try to think of ways we can improve. Come on guys. We are The Grounded Gang! WE CAN DO BETTER!

-Billy

> He seems very excited. Has he been drinking soda again? -Brain

> He drank four cans before he wrote this and it's not even lunchtime! -DD

Stuff for September

Roll Call

Smell of the Month

Secret Password for the Month

New Clubhouse Rules

Grounded……or Why I'm Not There

Scale of Injustice

Free Nelson Update

D.I.E. Update

Chickenbutt Bath Report

Stuff We Didn't Get Grounded for this Month

Grounded Central

Grounded Gang Money

Final Thoughts

Assignments for Next Month

Smell of the Month

I noticed that the base is starting to smell bad. So I've decided that each month we should take it in turns to bring in something to freshen things up a little. I've gone first. I brought in the car air freshener from my Dad's car. Now the place smells like 'Spicy Coconut Forest'. You're welcome. Gutsy, your turn next month…..no butts!

Secret Password for the Month

From now on nobody will be allowed to enter the base unless they give the secret password first. You cannot use any of the following instead:

- Abracadabra
- I forgot the password
- Open sesame seed bun
- Oh come on, you know it's me!
- Ding-dong
- We've known each other since we were five. Now, open the door!!!!
- Funky chicken
- Right, this is stupid, I'm going home.

This month's password will be:

TEA CHAIRS R CRAY ZEE

New Clubhouse Rules

Isn't that what the little tree is for? -DD

As a gang, we have to move with the times and stay fresh. So every month, we all get an opportunity to write any new rules we want to see. Then, we vote on it. If it's a tie I pick who wins....So let's see what everyone wants! Oh, and if the rule is dumb I get to cross it out, because I'm the President!

Rule	YES	NO
If you fart in the secret base and someone says, "who farted?" You have to own up! -DD	✓✓✓✓	✓✓
If you open the base fridge and see a sandwich that someone has written their name on, you cannot open it, take a bite, lick it, peel it open or eat the good bits. -Gutsy	✓✓✓✓✓	✓✓
Girls should be allowed to join the gang! -Billy	✓	✓✓✓✓✓✓✓
If someone accidentally forgets to wear underwear to a meeting, no-one is allowed to mention it or make jokes about it for the rest of my life! -Rock	✓✓	✓✓✓✓✓✓✓✓

What the heck!? -DD

Errrr....my bad! I must have written that by mistake. -Billy

Oh come on! There's not even that many of us in the gang! -Rock

Grounded….or why I'm not there!

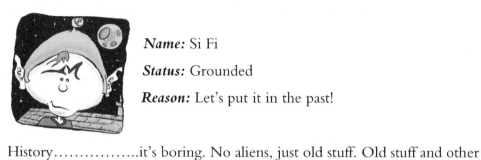

Name: Si Fi

Status: Grounded

Reason: Let's put it in the past!

History……………..it's boring. No aliens, just old stuff. Old stuff and other stuff that's already happened. Stuff from before computers were invented…. which, was when all the fun stuff began! They should have a special rule for the really boring classes like history. Something that lets you have three yawns every hour or a naptime if the teacher talks for more than 20 minutes. To make it worse, The Rattle was teaching History that day. The usual teacher was out sick so he'd agreed to 'help out'. We all knew that him 'helping out' with History was trouble. First, it meant him reading, which always makes him angry. Second, it meant a full hour where he wasn't allowed to make anyone do press ups, which always stresses him out!

So, we're 15 minutes into class and everything started to go wrong.

He was trying to teach us about evolution. Apparently, they thought that humans used to be monkeys or something like that? Anyway, some people said this wasn't true. I think these people had never spent an hour in a room with The Rattle. That would have made anyone realize that monkeys are actually much, much cleverer than certain humans!

So, The Rattle decided to draw us a picture of how monkeys slowly turned into humans, over like a million, billion years or something like that! But his drawing of a monkey looked more like a pirate, which made half the class think that all humans used to have wooden legs and eye patches. So, then he decided it would be better if someone else drew the picture for him instead. Admittedly, this next bit was my fault, as right at that moment I was lost in a daydream about playing video games in a giant seat made out of marshmallow. You know, so when you're hungry you could just lean over and eat one of the cushions....without having to stop playing?

Genius! - Gutsy   Best idea.......EVER! -Rock   We should make these and sell them? We'd be millionaires! -Billy

Anyway, the trouble started when I came out of my daydream and saw that everyone was pointing at me to go draw the picture. Now, I had no choice.

Rookie mistake! If you're not paying attention, then you will always get picked. That's classroom law. -DD

So, I did it. I got up there and did the best picture I could, even though I couldn't draw either! Anyway, I finished, I stood back from the board, I looked at my picture of a monkey....and I wished I was dead! I swear I never meant it. I could have drawn that picture a thousand times and it would never come out that perfect again. You see there, above the word 'MONKEY' I had managed to draw a perfect picture of The Rattle! And I'm not talking just a good drawing, I mean, it was perfect. If his own mother had walked in she would have said, "That's my son, the monkey!"

Nobody said a thing. I looked over at The Rattle and saw that he hadn't noticed yet as he was too busy looking longingly out the window at the football field, like he was missing his one true love. I knew I had to do something quick. I looked for the board eraser but I couldn't find it. So, I decided to draw some extra bits to make it look less like him. Only now all of the amazing drawing skills I had 2 seconds ago had left me. I tried to draw a different moustache but it looked like two big thick boogers coming out of his nose. I drew some glasses but they looked like two giant pimples. I tried to cross the whole thing out but all the lines just looked like whiskers. That's when I felt his hand on my shoulder……just as I had finished my perfect drawing of what The Rattle would look like if he was a kitten with a really bad cold and acne!

No surprises on what happened next.

He sent me to the Principal's office where The Hammer was looking at a picture on his phone….and it was only a photo of my drawing! The D.I.E. Sisters had taken it and sent it to him……………along with every kid/teacher/living thing in school………and some people not in our school…………like my Mom and Dad….along with the message, "Look what Si Fi did in school today!"

Outcome: I'm grounded for two weeks. It would have been a week but The Hammer persuaded my parents that an extra week would be better!

Si Fi's Grounding.... The Scale of Injustice

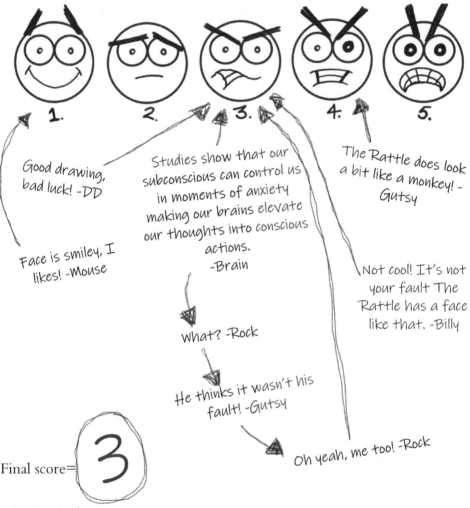

Injustice Scale

1- Dude, you were totally wrong. You deserve the grounding.

2- Alright, it was a mistake. But, dude, you were still wrong.

3- Well that wasn't cool, was it? They didn't have to ground you for that.

4- Whoa, that's totally not right. You don't deserve to be grounded for that.

5- WHAT!? That's not fair. Stay where you are, we're coming to get you.

Grounded....or why I'm not there!

Name: Mouse

Status: Grounded

Reason: Talking Trashcan Toilet

So, I have being practising my Eenglish and me am getting very much gooder, no? Goood. So, first me will be thank in you for letting me be in you gang. Me lick it very much. So, it is making me sad that I am not at meeting two day. But is not my bad. I have been, how you say...grinded? I am being at school one day when me needing to use the bathroom. Me is drinking two much of the soda you all lick so much. It is vely good. In my country we do not have soda, we is only allowed to drink milk from donkey. This is not tasting lick soda. It is tasting lick, how you say............how fart would taste if it coming out of hairy animal in field? Me no want to drink milk any more. Me want only soda. But soda is so good that I need to pee very much all the time.

So, I is at school, needing to go toilet, and I go into room with big red door

I think we just found out why we keep running out of soda! -Billy

that is bathrooms me think. First thing me thinks is how strange this bathroom is as is full of teachers. I waiting for one of thems to says somethings to me but me think they is all two bizzy to notice me because they is all looking at something on table.

They all is very xcited by thing they is looking at, as they is beings very loud and waving arms. Even all the cats that is there is ignores me. But no one is

What? -Brain

Chickenbutt! -Si Fi

still noticing me and me is needing to go the toilets so bad that I knows I cannot waits much longer. But this bathroom not likes the normals bathroom I find in yours countrys. There is no toilets. Only couches and kitchens. I am thinking this must be very fancy bathroom. Not like bathrooms from my village. In my village we don't have toilet. We is going outside where donkeys live or if is cold we use bucket. Me is needing to go pees very much bad now but is no time to go outside. Is emergency. I have to use bucket by table. Me go overs to bucket and see it is not like normal toilet bucket. This bucket full of paper. Then I see that paper has namez on it. Namez of all of us. The namez of the grinded gang. I is wanting to get the paper to shows alls of yous but me has to go pees reals bad now so I has to go in bucket befores me can get list. Bucket is very noisy when me go pee. This make teachers stop talking. They all stop looking at thing on table and turns to look at me.

They is all there. The Hammers, The Laws, The Needles, The Mops, The Gases, The Rattles. All is seeing me go pees.

Me no minds. At homes I is used to donkeez watching me go pee so is no big deal. But teachers thinks is big deal. Alls starts to scream at me. The Mops is only one not shouting. He is bizzy grabbing things from table before I can see whats it is they was all looking at. Then he starts shouts at me two. But is too late. I cannot stop. I have to goes pees so theys haves to wait for me's to finish. Now I wish I did not haves to stop peeing as I knows they will bees very angrys with me. So I remememberz what D.I.E. Sisters tell me to say if ever teacher is angry with me and I want to make them nots angry.

"You is ugly with face like dumpster full of diapers."

Who left him alone with the D.I.E. Sisters?!
-DD

D.I.E. Sisters says this is great compliment to says to someone in your country. Teachers no seems to thinks so. They is makings me go to Prettypals office and calling meyes parents. This is very expensive call to only phone in my village but teachers no care. They talks to meyes parents and when I gets on phones meyes parents says I is big trouble and that whens I gets home they is going to change my room into place for sheep to sleep and that I is grinded for 3 weeks. Nows I is missing meeting which is makings me sad. Only good thing is when teachers is shoutings they no sees me get list from bucket. I think mays be help to find outs why teachers no like us so much. Paper is little wet still but is okay. I hope it is helping. Also I is suggesting no body is smelling this paper. Is smelling real bad.

Grounded Evidence #1:

Also known as a peed on piece of paper! -Gutsy

Nelson..................Risk Level 5........Currently neutralized.
Mildred................Risk Level 3........Currently neutralized.
Billy......................Risk Level 5........Under surveillance.
Brain....................Risk Level 4........One to watch.
DD........................Risk Level 3........Lacks intelligence.
Mouse..................Risk Level 3........Smarter than he looks.
Si Fi....................Risk Level 4........Approach with caution.
Rock.....................Risk Level 1........No threat.
Gutsy....................Risk Level 3........Becoming curious.
Drool....................Risk Level 4........High intelligence.
Chickenbutt......Risk Level 4........Threat to the Master.

Why is the dog a higher risk level than me? -Rock

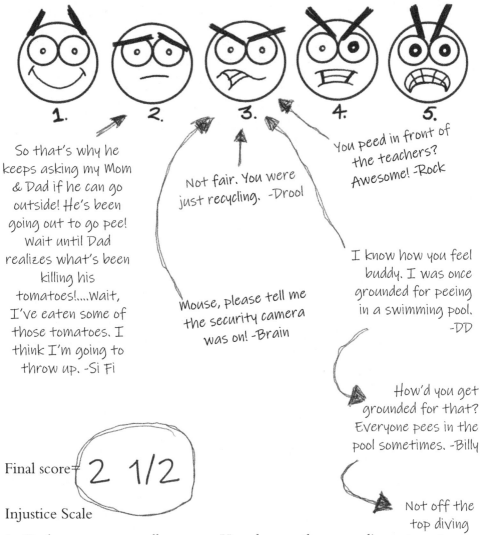

Free Nelson Update

Days Grounded: 242

DD and Rock, it was your job to find out more about why our leader is still grounded. What did you discover? Please tell me you got me us some of his Mom's homemade cookies!

Free Nelson Report by DD: We set up surveillance on Nelson's house and sat there every chance we had for 4 weeks. Unfortunately there were no sightings of Nelson. We did notice that his Mom is looking really old and she has cats that she talks to all day. That's all we found out. Sorry guys.

Did Nelson's old-looking Mom have red hair and wear lots of make-up? -Billy

Yep!- Rock

That's Nelson's next door neighbor! You were watching the wrong house! -Billy

What? Rock said he was 100% sure it was Nelson's house! -DD

So you spent four weeks looking at the wrong house? -Billy

Oooops! -Rock

Oooops!!!! 4 weeks wasted and he says oooops! -DD

So....just to check....no cookies then? -Billy

D.I.E. Update

Danni   Isabelle   Emily

Okay, let's start by finding out what D.I.E. have done to us this month.

	Wedgies	Stole my Stuff	Took embarrassing photos of me	Put gross stuff on me
Billy	✓		Picking nose	✓
Brain		✓		✓
DD				✓
Mouse				
Si Fi	✓ ✓			
Rock				✓
Gutsy	✓		Eating out of trash	
Drool				
Chickenbutt				

D.I.E Total = **11**

D.I.E Update....(continued)

Well, that was embarrassing! It's a good job we had a team spending the entire month following D.I.E. With their information we'll soon have revenge!

D.I.E. Report by Brain, Si Fi & Mouse:

What do D.I.E. call brooms?....Transportation!

Thank-you.

That's it! That's all that you have after 4 weeks? -Billy

It's not my fault! Si Fi and Mouse were grounded so I was on my own! I followed D.I.E. for nearly 20 minutes before they saw me. They used my underwear to clean my glasses....while I was wearing them! -Brain

So you thought we wouldn't notice that you didn't find anything out if you distracted us with a joke? -Billy

If the #2 pencil is the most popular pencil then why is it still #2? -Brain

Yeah....you can stop now. -Billy

Chickenbutt's Bath Report by Drool

Chickenbutt before his bath.

Me, before giving Chickenbutt a bath.

Stuff We Didn't Get Grounded For....

I thought it would do us good if we had a section where we could write anything that we didn't get grounded for this month. You know, to get rid of any guilt that we have for not being good.

What is guilt? -Mouse  No clue, Never heard of it! -DD

- We had a game of food baseball in the school bathroom. We used an apple for a ball. It was awesome....until we lost the apple! -DD, Si Fi, Mouse

- I found an apple in the toilet at school and took it to the canteen and swopped it for a new one....Drool

- I saw Gas throwing out apples from the canteen and I took them. -Rock

Rock, what did you do with the apples? -Billy

I put them in the base. -Rock

So, one of us has eaten an apple that was in the school toilets? -Brain

1. I don't see the problem.
2. The Gas throws away food where exactly?
3. Are there any apples left?
   Gutsy

Final Thoughts

Well guys, The Grounded Gang is definitely back! Okay, it wasn't our finest month but maybe we're just out of practice? Next month we'll be great! We'll find out what's going on with all the teachers, we'll defeat DIE, and we'll finally free Nelson! I can feel it! Next month is our month!

Okay guys, assignments are on the next page. Don't forget that next month is also Halloween, which means one thing! CANDY!!! Just in time too! We really need to replenish our supplies. This year Brain will be in charge of trick or treat assignments, and he's promised to include Nelson's house on our list of targets. It'll be a good opportunity for us all to learn where he lives. It's going to be tough for us to beat last years haul, when we collected enough candy for the next six months....but I believe in us!

We can do it Grounded Gang!

Okay, I'll see you all around base, but until next month's meeting, watch out for each other....and let's be careful out there, and if you can't be careful, be clever, and if you can't be clever....be Rock....let's just all be careful.

Don't think I've forgiven you yet Rock! -DD

What for? Oh yeah. Oooopps! -Rock

Too much soda again? -Brain

Yep, 4 cans before he wrote this! -DD

Assignments for Next Month

Project Free Nelson: Brain and Gutsy. See what you can find out. Don't forget to go to the right house this time. ⟵ ....and get cookies! -Billy

Drinks + Snacks: Drool.

Give Chickenbutt a Bath: Rock. ⟵ Good luck with that! -Drool

Protect the Base: Chickenbutt....maybe this is asking too much of you? How about you just try to stay awake for more than ten minutes and stop farting in your sleep. Good boy/whatever you are! You're a great mascot!

The Rest: Why don't you guys see if you can get us an update on the D.I.E. Sisters? Find out what you can....without getting any wedgies! It seems D.I.E. are getting rather good at them!

Grounded Gang Out!

Gutsy   Rock   DD   Drool

Mouse   Si Fi

Billy   (Chickenbutt)

Does Billy know Chickenbutt can't read? I think he's going a little crazy! - Gutsy

This is Chickenbutt. Not only can I read but I can write too! -Chickenbutt

WOW! Sorry Chickenbutt. I didn't know you were such an amazing dog. WOW! -Gutsy

Just kidding! I wrote that! But who's the crazy one now? -Billy

October

October Meeting

Letter from the President,

Where do I start? Well I think it goes without saying that it's been a bad month. More of us grounded….our candy and soda supplies dangerously low……and of course there's…..well, I don't even want to talk about that until I have to!

The only good thing happening to us right now is that tonight is the last night of October….and that means one thing! Halloween! Which means one more thing: trick or treating….and if there's one more thing The Grounded Gang does better than anyone else, it's trick or treating! We know the best neighborhoods, we have the best outfits, we do the best planning. Its like taking candy from a baby……..well, that's not true because tonight the only person we're not taking candy from is a baby!

Let's have a good meeting guys, and remember, don't let anything that is said in today's meeting bring us down. In fact, if anyone says anything we don't like, you know, perhaps some sort of bad news, let's all promise to not even think about it. In fact, that's a great idea! If anyone has any bad news, we shouldn't even really think about it….at all! We should just get on with it, forgive them, and concentrate on trick or treating. Yeah, that's what we should do. We should concentrate on trick or treating…………go candy!

-Billy

Dude! You are getting weirder and weirder -DD

Grounded Gang Central

My butt is the password, why? -Rock

Here's something new! I call it GROUNDED GANG CENTRAL! I converted one of the base windows into a noticeboard that tells us how we're doing each month! -Billy

Stuff for October

Roll Call

Secret Smell of the Month

Password for the Month

(Special Announcement) — *Change of plan! Let's move this down here and do it later in the meeting instead. -Billy*

New Clubhouse Rules

Grounded…….or Why I'm Not There

Scale of Injustice

Free Nelson Update — *Eeerr. Maybe it can wait a little longer. Let's do it here instead! -Billy*

D.I.E. Update

Chickenbutt Bath Report

Stuff We Didn't Get Grounded For This Month

Final Thoughts

Assignments for Next Month

Special Announcement — *Okay, no more changes! Let's do it here instead! -Billy*

Rollcall

(who's here!)

	Here	GROUNDED!
Nelson		✗
Billy	✓	
Brain	✓	
Double Dare		✗
Mouse	✓	
Si Fi	✓	
Rock		✗
Gutsy	✓	
Drool	✓	
Chickenbutt		

Is this the sort of stuff you lot do all the time?

Secret Smell of the Month

Who is this????
-Brain

Hi Guys, this is Gutsy, and this month I wanted to come up with a smell we'd all appreciate. So I went with….cheeseburgers! That's right, every day this month I put half a cheeseburger down the side of the couch releasing the sweet smell of cheese, ketchup, beef and pickles into our base. It's a food and an air freshener! And they call it junk food! Mouse, your turn next month but good luck beating this idea! ……Right, all this talking about cheeseburgers has made me hungry again. I'm off to lick the couch cushions.

I is finding and eating some of these air fresheners last weeks! They is good but me no likes the green furry parts so much. -Mouse

Password for the Month

This month's password will be:

ROCK SPOT HUM

Again, I would like to make an official complaint that my butt is the password! -Rock

New Clubhouse Rules

Remember guys, keep an open mind about ALL new club rules. We need to see the good in every new idea. We definitely should not get mad at anyone who comes up with an idea that makes you think 'that's crazy' or 'I want to kill him!' We should be kind and only show love....lots of love! Can you all agree to do that? In fact, why don't we go ahead and make that a new rule? Anyone suggesting a rule that seems dumb will only be treated nicely.... really nicely. There, don't you all feel better now?

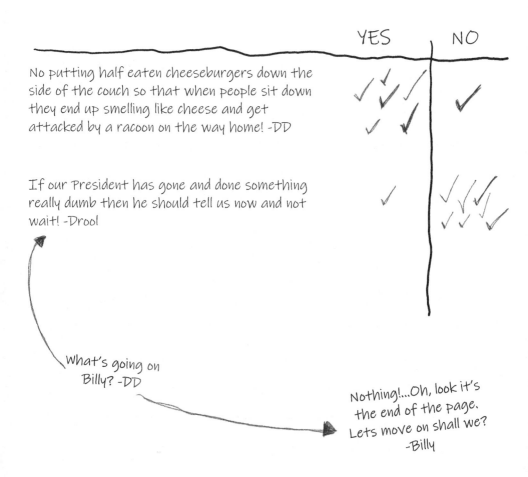

	YES	NO
No putting half eaten cheeseburgers down the side of the couch so that when people sit down they end up smelling like cheese and get attacked by a racoon on the way home! -DD	✓✓✓✓✓	✓
If our President has gone and done something really dumb then he should tell us now and not wait! -Drool	✓	✓✓✓✓✓

What's going on Billy? -DD

Nothing!...Oh, look it's the end of the page. Lets move on shall we? -Billy

Grounded....or why I'm not there!

Name: Double Dare

Status: Grounded

Reason: I was attacked by a bush/monster/teacher.

I never wanted to go. Mom made me. Apparently, I "can't be trusted on my own!" All because I once tried to take a bath in the washing machine when they both had to work late! So, while Mom and Dad were out on a date, I had to go to Gutsy's spooky walk party thingy. Now, I mean no offence when I say this Gutsy, but your Mom and Dad have been throwing that spooky walk party for years....and it's kinda dumb. With a capital 'O'.... dumbO! I mean it was cool when we were little kids but, freezing to death while we wait for your Dad to jump out of a bush just doesn't cut it as scary anymore. I was more scared the time he opened the door wearing just his underpants! But I had no choice. Mom said I had to go, so there I was, dressed as a skeleton, knocking on the door of the world's dumbOest spooky

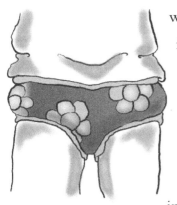

walk. Now, I know what you're all thinking: if it's so dumbO, how did I manage to get myself grounded? So, here's the thing, the party was different this year. You see it wasn't quite so dumbO. In fact for a scary party it was kinda.....scary. For example, I'm used to getting there and being greeted by Gutsy's Mom dressed in her usual terrible ghost costume.

But this year she'd really gone to town. She looked so freaky with these bulging bloodshot eyes, huge teeth, and this big wart on her nose.

> That was my Grandma! And she wasn't wearing a costume!
> -Gutsy

....awkward! -DD

"Quickly," she said, "you're the last one to arrive....we've been waiting for you."

Before I could speak she dragged me through the house and pushed me out into the backyard where I found myself standing next to a vampire, a pirate, a dinosaur, batman, and a mummy. Even weirder, I didn't know any of them.

Everyone was nervous about what was going to happen. Nobody was talking and there was a faint smell of pee in the air. So, I went up to this werewolf and asked him, "what's going on?" "It's the teachers," he whispered to me. "It's not just Gutsy's Dad being dumbO and jumping out of a bush like usual. This year it's the teachers all dressed up!"

> He did not say it was usually dumbO! -Gutsy

Now, I knew this couldn't be good, and I was about to leave, when this big zombie hand appeared on my shoulder. "Come along children," said The Mop. "Time to go for a walk through the woods." Next thing I knew we're being herded down this dark pathway. At that moment I'd have given anything for it just to be one of Gutsy's parent's usual dumbO parties. In fact, if Gutsy's

Dad had jumped out of a bush in just his underpants, I'd have been so happy I think I would have hugged him! ———▶ Oh, come on! -Gutsy

But there was no escape. All we could do was shuffle farther and farther into the darkness as Zombie Mop shouted at us to move faster.

The pathway seemed to be getting smaller and smaller. The trees seemed to be getting bigger and bigger. The darkness seemed to be getting thicker and thicker. The smell of pee seemed to be getting stronger and stronger.

Then, we heard it. The bushes started to growl.

Well, I can tell you, we didn't think twice. We took off running down the path, deeper and deeper into the woods, which seemed a good idea at the time, as it was away from the growling!

In front of me, Dracula was running as fast as he could and judging by the smell he was leaving behind he was even more scared than me! On and on we ran but it was no use, the growling was gaining on us! Between the trees we started to see flashes of sharp white teeth and yellow eyes! Faster and faster we ran, leaving behind bits of costume and a smell like the school bathrooms after taco's for lunch. ▶ I have try this taco lunch. After is like I am pooping firework! -Mouse

Then, we saw it....a car coming toward us with bright headlights and a roaring engine! The Werewolf kid was the first one to run toward it and the rest of us were only just behind; all of us waving our arms for it to stop. (Which just seemed to spread the really bad smell even more let me tell you!) Only, the car wasn't slowing down, instead it was getting faster! And the growling was getting louder! And the pirate next to me started screaming and in that moment we realized that the car was going to hit us!

Suddenly, something bumped against my leg and I looked down to see that the kid in the dinosaur costume has fainted with fear.

Dudes, he probably passed out because he was young. Only little kids wear dinosaur costumes -Si Fi

It's true. I'm 6 and I wouldn't wear a dinosaur costume anymore. It must have been a little kid. -Drool

In a panic I searched for a way to escape but, the only way out was blocked by this big bush. A bush with bright yellow eyes, long tentacles, and big sharp teeth! All I could hear was the roar of the car engine and kids screaming all around me. So, I did the only thing I could think of. I picked up a big stick and shouted for the others to follow me. Then, I ran toward the bush and started hitting it as hard as I could....over and over!

Now, this was where it got quiet real quick! But I wasn't really paying attention as I was too busy hitting the bush. Then, it suddenly wasn't so dark anymore. But I kept hitting. Then, the screaming stopped altogether. But I kept hitting. Even the smell didn't seem quite so bad. I gave it one last hit.

That's when I looked up and saw The Law and The Hammer standing there holding a piece of wood with two big flashlights tied to it, and The Gas is standing next to them holding a stereo that was playing the sound of a car engine. Slowly, I realized it wasn't a car at all. It was just them pretending to be a car to scare us. And then I realized that if the car was fake then....I looked down at the monster, in the bush, I was trying to kill.

Only there was no monster.

It was The Rattle, lying there with these two giant fake eyeballs strapped to his head. That's when I thought it would be a good idea to drop the stick. Only it went and landed on his foot and he let out this big scream like I'd shot him! That's when I felt the zombie hand on my shoulder again!

"Time for you to have a talk with the Principal, I think!" said Zombie Mop.

Before I had a chance to think I was standing in Gutsys kitchen with The Law....who was on the phone to my Mom!

"....Then there's the fact that he hit Mr. Bulk even after he knew it was him!" he said to her, like I'd meant to drop the stick on his foot!

I wanted to shout out that I was actually a hero for trying to save the other kids but I knew it wouldn't do any good. Mom thinks all the teachers at our school can do no wrong, and, nothing I say is going to persuade her otherwise.

"I have to say," said The Law, "I think Chris needs to be taught a lesson. I would suggest a minimum of three weeks grounding, with additional homework, of course. He needs to be kept busy!"

Outcome: I've been stuck in my room since that day, doing extra homework. I need you all to come get me as it's pretty obvious that I didn't do anything wrong! I dare you not to rescue me! -DD

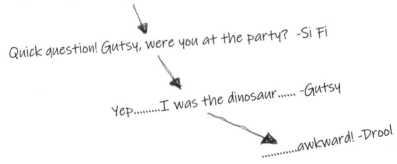

Quick question! Gutsy, were you at the party? -Si Fi

Yep.........I was the dinosaur...... -Gutsy

...........awkward! -Drool

Double Dare's Grounding....The Scale of Injustice

It's kinda hard to feel too bad for you. After all........
YOU WERE THE ONLY ONE OF US INVITED TO THE PARTY!
-Billy, Si Fi, Brain, Drool, Mouse, Rock

That wasn't really his fault. I wasn't allowed to invite the rest of you....my parents think you're all a bad influence on me. DD was invited because our Mom's are best friends and she said it was an emergency.
-Gutsy

What was the emergency? -Brain

His Mom said she'd kill him if she didn't get him out of the house!
-Gutsy

Final score = 3

Injustice Scale

1- Dude, you were totally wrong. You deserve the grounding.

2- Alright, it was a mistake. But, dude, you were still wrong.

3- Well, that wasn't cool, was it? They didn't have to ground you for that.

4- Whoa, that's totally not right. You don't deserve to be grounded for that.

5- WHAT!? That's not fair. Stay where you are, we're coming to get you.

Quick Meeting Break -Drool

Sorry to stop the meeting but I have something to tell you....I'm afraid I have good news and bad news. -Drool

What is it? Is everything okay? -Billy

Yeah, are you okay Drool? -Brain

The good news is I have decided to warn you that I'm about to fart
The bad news is I should have told you 10 seconds ago! -Drool

Oh man! I can't breathe! Quick, someone open a window.....Who boarded up the window and wrote all over it?....I'm dying! It smells like a toilet burped in here! -Si Fi

What is smelling so bad? What? What? -Mouse

Chickenbutt! -Gutsy

Nope. It was me! -Drool

Grounded….or why I'm not there!

Name: Rock

Status: Grounded

Reason: History is against me.

So, I'll begin by saying that I know I'm not the best student in school….but, I'm not as bad as they seem to think I am!

> I don't know about that. I once asked him what his I.Q. was. He asked me how to spell it! -Brain

Here's what happened. We had a pop quiz and I thought I did good. Only, next day I got called into The Hammer's office and he said I'm not taking school seriously. I asked him what he meant and he showed me my test paper which now had a big red 'F' at the top and lots of red kisses all over it. I thought about it and said that, while I was sure my teacher was a lovely lady, I'd rather she didn't send me anymore kisses. This seemed to make him really mad and he started shouting that they were crosses not kisses and that I'd scored a zero on the test.

So, I think he's going to say I have to do another test. But, instead he told me he'd arranged some extra help for me. That's when the D.I.E. Sisters walked in. It turned out they were the extra help!

So, for the next two weeks I have to sit in the school library everyday with one of the D.I.E. Sisters doing extra homework.

So far, I've only learnt three subjects:
1. PHYS ED – Danni will show you all the karate moves she knows if you ask her to explain why she has a boy's name. She's got a black belt. I've got a black eye.
2. MATH – Isabelle can give you three wedgies, two dead arms and one head lock in the time it takes the librarian to go to the bathroom.
3. CHEMISTRY – Emily knows how to do silent farts that are so bad they knock you unconscious. And when you wake up she can do another one almost instantly.

It's so unfair. I didn't do that badly on the test. Here I'll show you.

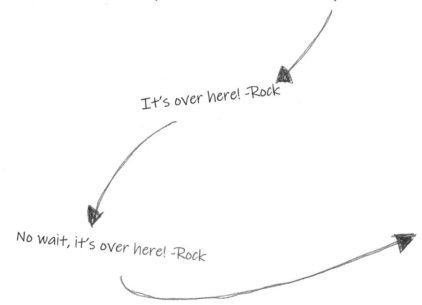

Grounded Evidence #2:

Here's some pages from my test. -Rock

Write your name here:
Your name here.

(a) Why did the Great Wall of China fail?

Most of it was great but there were bits of it that were just kinda good. And then there was this one bit called 'The Not Very Good at all Wall of China'. I read on the internet that it was made out of sticks and old gym socks, so when the enemy found that bit they knocked it down really easily. They just had to kick it and it fell over. I think they were ninjas. It sounds like something ninjas would do.

(d) What is the third world? Give details

Okay, so the world we live in is actually the second world! The first world was destroyed when a dinosaur ate the Queen Alien who ruled the earth back then. When the King Alien found out he was so mad that he used a laser to kill all the dinosaurs! Only it turned out that the Queen wasn't dead after all. She'd gone out shopping for some toilet paper on Uranus and when she got home and found out what he'd done she was really mad and made him make a new world, which is the one we call home. But what he didn't tell the Queen was that while he was making this world he made another secret one underground! It's where the 'secret people' live. Aliens keep them down there so they can use them as fuel for their spaceships. Of course the 'secret people' don't know this so they are all happy and stuff. Until the aliens come and put them in their gas tanks. This is all top secret of course. I only know it because my friend Si Fi told me all about it. He knows everything about aliens. So, it's true. I swear!

It is all true....well kind of! -Si Fi

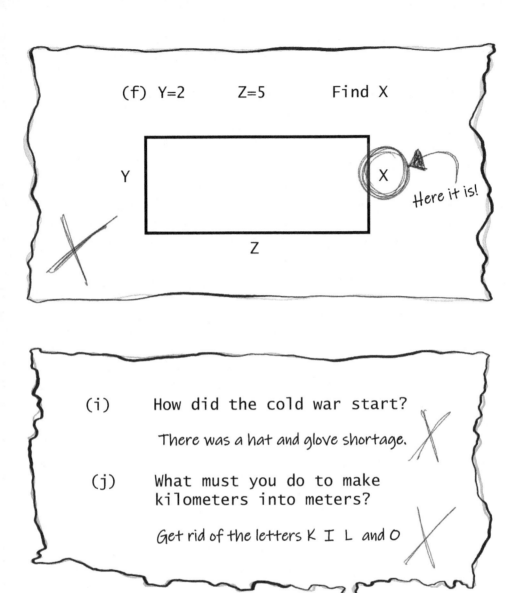

See! Just like I told you! I didn't do that bad. I'm starting to think that the teachers just don't like me……or any of us!

Outcome: Three weeks with the D.I.E. Sisters….Help me!

Rock's Grounding.... The Scale of Injustice

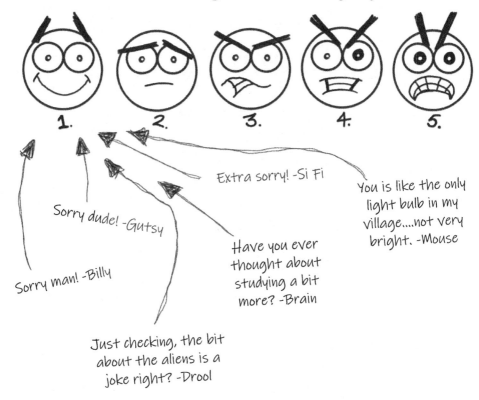

Injustice Scale

1- Dude, you were totally wrong. You deserve the grounding.

2- Alright, it was a mistake. But, dude, you were still wrong.

3- Well, that wasn't cool, was it? They didn't have to ground you for that.

4- Whoa, that's totally not right. You don't deserve to be grounded for that.

5- WHAT!? That's not fair. Stay where you are, we're coming to get you.

Free Nelson Update

by Brain & Gutsy

Days Grounded: 273

So, we had this genius idea to get into Nelson's house. First, Gutsy goes to the front door disguised as a delivery man and pretends he's there to deliver pizza. While he's doing that, I sneak in the back door and go find Nelson. Simple……… genius!

And in the beginning, the plan was working perfectly. Gutsy rang the doorbell and as soon as I heard the front door open I was in the back door and half-way up the stairs before anyone had a chance to notice. Downstairs I could hear Nelson's mom arguing that she hadn't ordered any pizza, while upstairs I could see Nelson's bedroom door….and it was wide open.

He's been grounded, not put in space prison! -Billy

No bars? No fences or lasers? No force fields? How strange. -Si Fi

The only thing between me and Nelson was an old, fat cat asleep on the top step. Suddenly the sound of Nelson's Mom arguing about the pizza rose to a whole new level of angry.

I snuck a peek over the top of the railing only to see Nelson's mom shouting at Gutsy as she pointed wildly at the inside of the pizza box.

I didn't know Nelson had a cat? -Billy

It seems that she was so desperate to get rid of him that she had decided to buy the pizza after all. Only, when she opened the box, she found a large pizza pie with several huge pieces already missing.

It seemed that someone, let's call him 'The one of us who was just supposed to deliver the pizza and not eat any of it in the ten seconds he was alone with it', had messed up our plan!

I only had a few seconds to decide what to do next. I knew I should run away; from the noises I was hearing it wasn't going to be long before Nelson's mom slammed the door in Gutsy's face. But I was so close, I just had to go on! I turned back, ready to make a run for his bedroom, only to find another problem. Old, fat cat wasn't asleep anymore. In fact, old, fat cat wasn't looking so old or fat anymore. Old, fat cat was now standing on his back legs, his claws out, looking more like a kung fu master! Instinctively I made a run for Nelson's bedroom, hoping to be too fast for old, fat cat. I was wrong.

> So during last months mission you were attacked by girls. This month you're running away from a cat. Not very....manly is it? - Billy

> 1. Girls are just as scary as boys!
> 2. Leave him alone!
> 3. Don't be so mean!
>
> WHO ARE YOU? -Brain

It seemed old, fat, kung-fu cat had taken some extra ninja lessons because in a single leap he back-flipped across the landing, cartwheeled into Nelson's doorway and, here's the really weird part, he leapt up and closed the door!

For a second I just stood there, open-mouthed at what I'd just seen. Then I realized something. I was trapped! Downstairs I heard Nelson's mom's voice, "Snuffy, are you okay? Is there something wrong?"

Old, fat cat looked at me. Then he did this weird thing with his mouth, like he was smiling, then he let out a long, "Mmmeeeeooooowww", that somehow sounded more like, "Killllllllllllll!"

The sound of Nelson's mom's footsteps on the stairs sent me into a panic. I went flying into the bathroom, where my heart flipped when I saw that the window was open! Before I could even think of what I was doing I was down the drain pipe and in the backyard, where Gutsy was waiting for me behind the fence.

The mission failed. Sorry guys.

Any luck with Nelson's mom's homemade cookies? -Billy

We got some! Brain grabbed some for you on his way into the house..........but I ate them! -Gutsy

Mission fail. -Billy

D.I.E. Update

Danni   Isabelle   Emily

Okay, let's start by finding out what D.I.E. have done to us this month.

	Wedgies	Stole my Stuff	Took embarrassing photos of me	Locked me in a supply closet
Billy				
Brain		✓	After I ripped my pants in gym	
DD		✓		
Mouse				
Si Fi				
Rock	✗✓✗✓			✓
Gutsy			Eating out of trash	
Drool				✓
Chickenbutt				

D.I.E Total= **15**

D.I.E Update.........continued by Mouse with DD and SiFi

Is very funny. I is liking this assignment. We is following D.I.E. sisters to their secrets base in middle of graveyards. When they is leavings we is followings as we wants to steals key to get into their secrets base. But is very boring following D.I.E. All they do is walk and walk. We is about to gives up for day when D.I.E. sisters sit on bench in park. Si Fi dares Double Dares to go steal the key. Is very dangerous mission and he is saying no but SiFi is doubles darings him so he is saying yes! Double Dares is saying this is laws! If someone is double darings you then you is having to say yes!

So, D.I.E. Sisters is sitting on bench and Double Dare is crawlings up behind them. They no see him coming! Slowly, he is takings something out of D.I.E. Sister's pocket and we is thinking he has dones it! Then we see that Double Dares is looking very ~~funny~~ scared. When D.I.E. Sisters gets up and walks away we go see what is wrong. Double Dares is no able to moves as big spiders is in his hand! He is taking D.I.E. Sisters pet tarantula by mistakes! He is very much freakings out but he has to wait for tarantulas to walk off his hand as he no wants it to bites him! Spider is sitting there for very longs time. We no finding out anything about D.I.E. Sisters but me and SiFi is laughing so much I thinks me might pees pants!

I did! (Just a little bit) -Si Fi

2 hours it took for that stupid spider to leave.....2 HOURS!....2 hours of watching you two laughing while I try not to get bitten....by a deadly spider! -DD

Chickenbutt Bath Report by Rock

Chickenbutt before his bath

Chickenbutt after his bath

Me, telling Chickenbutt I was about to give him a bath.

How I must have looked to Chickenbutt when I told him I was about to give him a bath. I know this because he began barking, bit me, sat on my head, farted, grabbed the chicken leg, and ran away!

Stuff We Didn't Get Grounded For

- I may, or may not, have snuck into the canteen during recess and licked old food off the serving trays when I was hungry. -Gutsy

- I killed a man. -Mouse

- Okay....I definitely did sneak into the school canteen during recess....and I definitely did lick old food off some serving trays....76 to be exact ...and I definitely wasn't hungry. (I'd just had a huge breakfast). -Gutsy

- Sorry, sorry, me English still no so good. I killed a HAM is what I is meaning. I is finding old ham sandwich in base fridge and is eating it. -Mouse

Ham sandwich....in the base fridge....he killed Percy! -Billy

What? Who is Percy? -Drool

First of all, you're a Chickebutt!....Secondly, Percy was our gang sandwich. He was left in the fridge at our first meeting and we've had him ever since....he was like family! -Billy

Now I is feeling bad. -Mouse

That's okay Mouse. You didn't know. -Billy

No. I mean I is feeling bad. Me thinks I is going to throws up! -Mouse

Final Thoughts by Billy

Okay guys, good meeting! So maybe it wasn't our best month:

    D.I.E. seem to keep getting the best of us.

    The teachers seem to hate us more and more everyday.

    We still haven't completed any of our assignments successfully.

    Chickenbutt still hasn't had a bath.

    We are running dangerously low on soda and candy.

    We have very little money left.

But let's not get down! We've had some successes....there was the....oh yeah, that didn't work. What about when we.....no, that ended badly too. Ah ha! Now I remember....I totally forgot that we....oh that's right. That was a complete nightmare.

Okay, so not the best month. But we still have trick or treat tonight! Nothing makes things better than a belly full of candy....especially when it's free candy! Let's be positive and not feel bad!

Tonight is the night that we turn it all around! In fact, let's feel good about that. And as long as we're feeling good, let's just treat each other the same way. After all, we've been friends since kindergarten, so if one of us were to do something that the others didn't like well maybe we should just be kind to them. Friends forever! -Billy

He gets weirder....and weirder....and weirder! -Brain

Assignments for Next Month

D.I.E. Update: Drool, Gutsy and....ME! It's time for you all to watch a real man take control of those sisters!

YES!....Oh wait! He's talking about himself....yeah, that's not going to end well.... -Gutsy

Project Free Nelson: Rock, Mouse. This one's all you guys! We know security is tight but, you saw how close Brain and Gutsy got! Try again, I believe in you!

Drinks + Snacks: DD & Si Fi. With the mountain of candy we will be bringing back to base tonight, you guys are going to be busy!

Give Chickenbutt a Bath: Brain, your turn. Be brave.

Protect the Base: Chickenbutt....maybe this is asking too much of you? How about you just try to stay awake for more than ten minutes and stop farting in your sleep? Good boy/whatever you are! You're a great mascot!

Grounded Gang Out!

Gutsy *Rock* *DD* *Drool*

Mouse *Si Fi*

Billy *(Chickenbutt)*

Special Announcement by Billy

Okay guys. Well I have some news….I don't really know how to tell you this but, I've accepted a new member into the gang. Their membership card is on the next page. Before you look, I just ask that you try to keep an open mind….and be nice when you find out who it is….especially to me.
I will be ~~running away~~ leaving now. You may not see me around the base very much for a few days but, I promise, I will explain everything at the next meeting….when you've all calmed down….I hope….please?

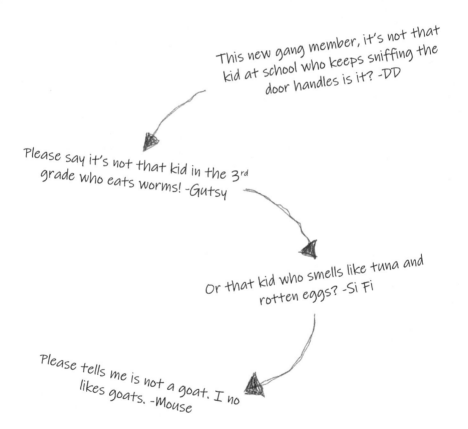

This new gang member, it's not that kid at school who keeps sniffing the door handles is it? -DD

Please say it's not that kid in the 3rd grade who eats worms! -Gutsy

Or that kid who smells like tuna and rotten eggs? -Si Fi

Please tells me is not a goat. I no likes goats. -Mouse

Lou Lou

Age: 11

Longest Grounding: Recently grounded for 2 weeks for the first time in her life....and she is not happy about it, let me tell you!!!!

WHAT!   WHAT!   WHAT!

GROUNDED GANG MEMBER

Name: Lou Lou Skipster

Codename: Code names are for silly boys. Lou Lou is my name. Please use it.

Skills: Being better than boys

Secret Smell: 〰️〰️

WHAT!   WHAT!   WHAT!

Oooohhhhh! I read about this in the rules! I think this is where I have to call you all a name....
You are all CHICKENBUTTS!
....You know? That was fun! -Lou Lou

Couldn't we get that kid who keeps sniffing the door handles instead? -DD

What about worm boy? Maybe he's available? -Gutsy

Don't forget tuna and egg boy. I'm sure we could get used to the smell? -Si Fi

She is not goat is she? -Mouse

November

Billy....A GIRL?!?!....WHY??????

Can we ground Billy for this? -DD

November Meeting

Letter from The President:

Okay, I get it, you're all mad at me. But come on, it's been four weeks already! Isn't it time for you all to forgive me? I did something you didn't like when I let a girl join the gang. Then you did some things I didn't like when you started calling me a girl, told everyone at school I'd changed my name to Belinda and sent my Mom a card congratulating her for having a new baby girl.

So, can we be even already? *← Not even close Belinda! -Si Fi*

And, if we're not even yet, can I at least get a chance to explain?

Look, I didn't want her to join the gang. When she first stopped me and said she wanted to be a part of our gang I laughed so hard I peed my pants. Fortunately we were in swim class at the time.

But the next day, she came up to me again. Only this time, she said if I didn't let her join the gang then she was going to show everyone something. Then she gave me a photo from when we were little. Now, I really don't want to do this but I'm going to put it on the next page for you all to see. I'm going to cover it up so no-one sees it by accident. You guys can look, BUT YOU CAN NEVER, NEVER, NEVER, NEVER SHOW ANYONE ELSE. I'm only letting you see because I trust you............and it's the only way to make you understand.

Be nice...........................

Eeeewwww. I'm in the swim class after yours. I swam in your pee! -Drool

106

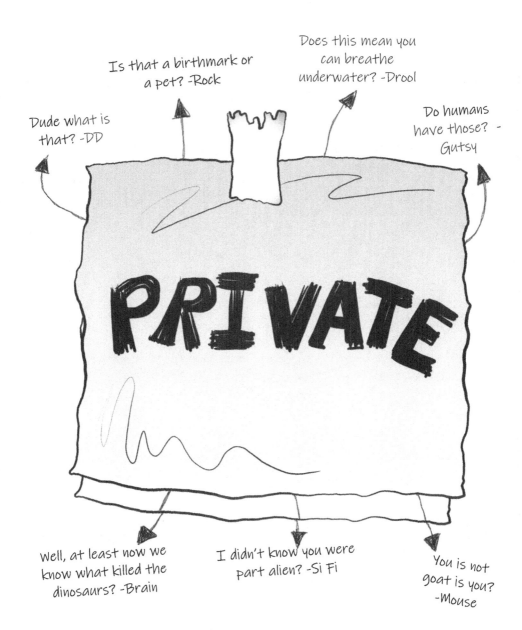

Oh, ha ha! Look, Lou Lou's Mom took that photo of me playing in her pool when I was two! And just for the record, lots of kids have it and it's nothing to be ashamed of! -Billy

 Your Mom told you that, didn't she? -DD   Yes. Billy

Now do you see why I had to do it????

If anyone at school ever saw what's under that flap I would never be able to show my face there again! I had to let her in The Grounded Gang!

I was as angry as you about it…..then last week she sent me a letter. Look guys, I didn't want her in the gang either but you really should read what she wrote.

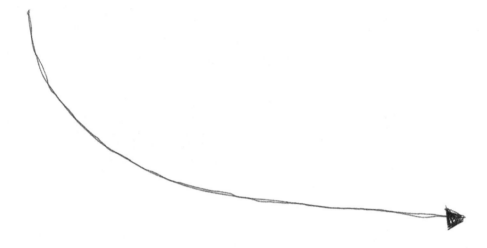

Nope, didn't notice a thing! -Gutsy

Dear Billy and The Grounded Gang,

I wanted to write to say thank-you for letting me be apart of your gang. I know none of you wanted me, especially as I blackmailed my way in but, I had no choice. We all live close to each other, we go to the same school, and I've seen what's been happening to all of you. How the teachers keep picking on you and how you all keep getting in trouble all the time? It's just not fair! Not that I really cared….at first! You are just boys after all! Then, a couple of months ago, it started happening to me too! I'm sure you noticed? The D.I.E. Sisters started picking on me and the teachers started being mean to me. Then last month I was grounded, for the first time in my life, for something I didn't do! It was so unfair!
Then, all of a sudden, I wasn't allowed to hang out with my friends anymore. Apparently, I'd become a "bad influence!"
Then, one day at school, I overheard some of you whispering about this Grounded Gang and how you're trying to work out how to stop getting grounded.
Look, I don't want to be in your stupid gang but I need your help to stop getting in trouble so I can get my friends back! And, having looked at how things are going for The Grounded Gang lately I think you could do with my help too. So, lets not argue. Let's just get on with trying to solve this problem so that we can all get back to our regular lives as soon as possible.
What do you say?

-Lou Lou

We'll be the judge of that, thank-you! -Brain

See what I mean? Look, I'm not saying we have to like her, but she might actually be useful to us. I mean she tricked her way into the gang so she must be clever….for a girl!

And it's not like things are going great for us right now!

The D.I.E. Sisters are killing us and you all remember how bad Halloween was! Let's face it guys, things are getting worse and we need some help. Anyway, it won't be for long. As soon as D.I.E. and the teachers are off our backs, she's history.

So, what do you say? Can we just give her a try? After a couple of months we'll have a vote, and if we really still don't want her then I'll ask her to leave the gang,…..even if it means she'll show everyone that picture.

I may have to go live on a desert island for the rest of my life but if that's what it takes to get you guys to forgive me, I'll do it.

So, what do you say? Can we give her a chance?

Dude, on the way to that island, you really need to stop at a doctors and get that thing looked at. -Si Fi

A Page For Your Thoughts....

-I don't know Billy. You make sense....but she's still a girl!! -DD

-I heard someone in my 1st grade class say that girls have a disease called cooties. I think it gives you diarrhea. -Drool

-Yeah, that's true Drool! Someone even wrote a song about it. It goes like this: 'Boys rule, girls give diarrhea to kids called Drool!' -Billy

-Look guys. I really don't like it either, but he has a point. Marie Curie, Clara Barton, Joan of Arc, Queen Bodecia. History is full of women who have done amazing things. If this girl can help us stop getting wedgies I think we should give her a chance. -Brain

-Yeah guys! I was just about to say that too. Marry Curry, Beg Your Pardon, Joan of the Lost Arc, Queen Diarrhea. All great women who can stop us getting wedgies. -Rock

-Do you know how insulting that was? Lou Lou

-No? Does he go to our school? -Rock

Girl Vote by Billy

I've decided to let you all vote on it. If you agree that Lou Lou should be given two months to prove herself worthy of being in The Grounded Gang, say yes. And if you think that Lou Lou should be asked to leave now, meaning she'll show everyone that picture and ruin my life forever, say no.

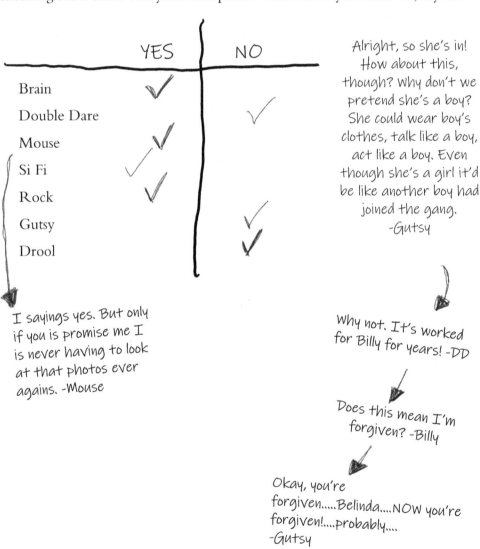

	YES	NO
Brain	✓	
Double Dare		✓
Mouse	✓	
Si Fi	✓	
Rock	✓	
Gutsy		✓
Drool		✓

I sayings yes. But only if you is promise me I is never having to look at that photos ever agains. -Mouse

Alright, so she's in! How about this, though? Why don't we pretend she's a boy? She could wear boy's clothes, talk like a boy, act like a boy. Even though she's a girl it'd be like another boy had joined the gang. -Gutsy

Why not. It's worked for Billy for years! -DD

Does this mean I'm forgiven? -Billy

Okay, you're forgiven.....Belinda....NOW you're forgiven!....probably.... -Gutsy

Grounded Gang Central

Stuff for November

Roll Call

Special Halloween Report ◄——— *Do we have to talk about it? It makes me want to cry! -Billy*

Secret Smell of the Month

Password for the Month

New Clubhouse Rules

Grounded…….or Why I'm Not There

Scale of Injustice

Free Nelson Update

D.I.E. Update

Chickenbutt Bath Report

Stuff We Didn't Get Grounded for this Month

Final Thoughts

Assignments for Next Month

Rollcall

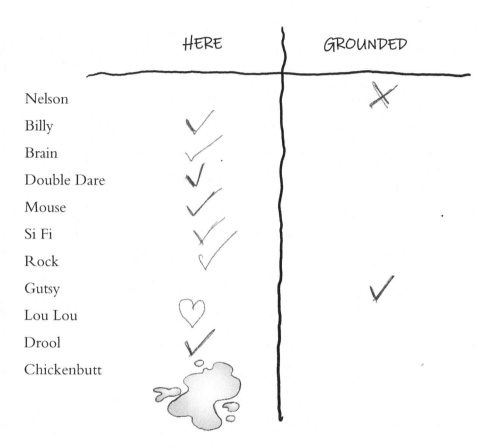

Special Halloween Report by Billy

Look guys, I know none of us want to think about that night again but I think it's important we put it in the book. If we're going to solve this problem we must look at all the facts. *Here's a fact. It was horrible! -Si Fi* And some really weird stuff happened that night. Things are getting bad guys. I know some kids are saying The Grounded Gang has a persecution complex but I'm telling you, someone….or something…..is out to get us all in as much trouble as possible. We have to put our heads together and look at everything. We need to work out why someone is out to get us, and we need to start with that night. Let's start at the beginning…………

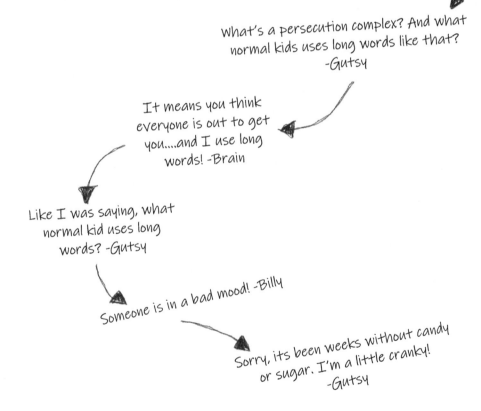

What's a persecution complex? And what normal kids uses long words like that? -Gutsy

It means you think everyone is out to get you….and I use long words! -Brain

Like I was saying, what normal kid uses long words? -Gutsy

Someone is in a bad mood! -Billy

Sorry, its been weeks without candy or sugar. I'm a little cranky! -Gutsy

Halloween Part 1- Our Plan by Brain

Also known as: Operation Sugar Rush

In charge: Brain

This is what we thought would happen! -Billy

Okay Grounded Gang, this is our big night so let's keep it simple. We just need to stick to the plan, follow orders, and get the candy! We've been working this neighborhood for years, it's our neighborhood. We've done our homework and nobody knows it better than us!

We're ready. So read the plan, then let's get out there and do our thing.

The Plan:

You'll soon see that you have all been divided into two teams. Team Cute and Team Gruesome. On the map you'll see that I have carefully divided the neighborhood between the two teams.

Team Cute: you will be focusing on houses belonging to old ladies and mothers. My studies have shown that kids in cute costumes get double the amount of candy from women compared to kids in regular costumes. So, keep those eyes wide, use lots of baby words, and say things like, "you look like a young version of my Mommy," or, "today is my birfday," as often as possible.

Team Gruesome: you will be visiting the homes of old men and fathers. Remember: don't be cute! My studies show that men will give double the amount of candy to kids who are willing to be quick! They don't want to talk, they want to give you the candy and get back to the T.V. as quickly as possible. So, knock on the door, say trick or treat, get the candy, and go.

It all seemed so simple! Where did it all go wrong? -Brain

Team Cute Outfits	Team Gruesome Outfits
Billy- Monkey	Si Fi- Alien
Rock - Teddy Bear	Gutsy –Grimm Reaper
Drool - Sheep	DD - Zombie
Mouse – Bunny Rabbit	Chickenbutt – Dog (this may be impossible)

You will notice I am not on either team. I will be operating the Trick or Treat Tactical Center from Billy's bike. In the equipment bags you will find a walkie-talkie. If you run into trouble, call me immediately. Time is candy guys.

Learn what to look for!

We only take candy on the approved list. If someone gives you candy from the unacceptable list be sure to place it in the bag marked 'CHICKENBUTT FOOD' upon return to base.

Acceptable	Unacceptable
Chocolate (milk or dark)	Toothbrushes
Anything 99% sugar (or greater)	Prunes/raisins
Anything that glows in the dark	Weird giant orange peanuts
	Root beer candy. –Rock

They taste like soap people! What do you think they are made of? Grown-up's are trying to get us to wash from the inside! -Rock

Equipment Bags

Each team will be given an equipment bag containing the following:

1 Can of soda. (Use only in need of an emergency sugar rush.)

1 Walkie talkie.

1 Can of Air Freshener. I borrowed some of the costumes from the dressing up box at my Mom's daycare center. They may be a little small....and not smell too good. Rock, your teddy bear costume was made for a three-year old. It will be tight, and you will be sweating.

Credit Card Machines – If they don't have any candy we are now able to accept all major credit cards instead.

Fake Signs- for people who just leave a bowl of candy on the doorstep.

Replace this................with this.

The Map

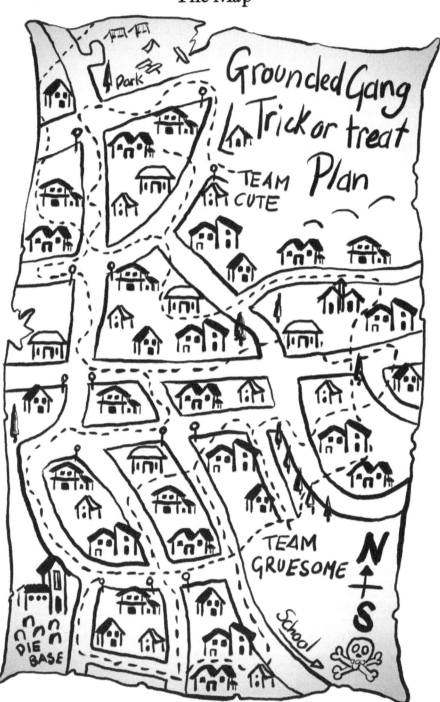

Final Thoughts

That's the plan guys. Stick to it and we'll have more candy than we know what to do with!

Final, Final Thoughts

1. Get in, get out. Time is candy.
2. Look good….or bad (check which team you're on first).
3. We accept candy or credit cards… no loose change!
4. We don't eat until the end.

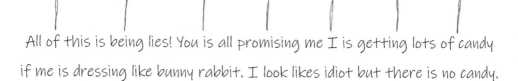

All of this is being lies! You is all promising me I is getting lots of candy if me is dressing like bunny rabbit. I look likes idiot but there is no candy. WHERE IS MY CANDY?? I WANTS MY CANDY……… and where is all soda going from base? ME IS NEEDING SODA! – Mouse

Oh, great! We've created a monster! -Billy

Halloween part 2-The Next Day by SiFi

Also known as: We're sugar free and not happy about it.

I'll be giving the second part of this report on behalf of Brain. What happened last night is too painful for him to write about. But I think we should start by thanking Brain for all his hard work. He put lots and lots of hours into creating the perfect trick or treating plan and the fact that we came back without even a single piece of candy was not his fault. It was all someone else's.... *HEY! I have a name! -Lou Lou*

We've all lived close to each other all our lives. Even the girl lives by us. And we've all known our neighbors since we were little. But yesterday that changed..........overnight. All of the neighbors we've all known for years disappeared, and in their place we got....'new neighbors'.

Our Old Neighbors	Who Lives in Their House Now
Mrs. Smith, age: 82	Mr. Hammer a.k.a. THE MALLET
Mrs. McGuire, age 79	Mrs. Tenison a.k.a THE LAW
The Sullivans, family of 4	Nurse Payne a.k.a NEEDLES
Mrs. Stevens, age 98	Mr. McTavy a.k.a. THE MOP
Mr. & Mrs. Jones, ages 78 and 80	Ms. Mulberry a.k.a. GAS
The Brown, family of 5	Mr. Bulk a.k.a. THE RATTLE

IT'S OUR ENEMIES....WE NOW LIVE
NEXT DOOR TO OUR ENEMIES!

If this wasn't bad enough they did it just in time to ruin Halloween! Every one of them now lives in a house that used to be owned by someone who gave us loads of candy every year! Mrs. Stevens used to give out three packs of big candy bars and Mr. Sullivan used to give homemade life-sized chocolate skulls! Those two alone kept us in the candy business for nearly a month! But now, sadly, they're gone.

This year everyone in our whole neighborhood wasn't home....except for our enemies. All the other neighbors were given free tickets to go the movies....by our enemies. And guess who didn't give out any candy this Halloween?....Our enemies.

Name	What They Gave Us
The Mallet	A lecture.
The Law	A pop quiz.
Needles	A vitamin shot.
The Mop	Toilet paper and hand sanitizer.
The Rattle	Laps around the block.
Gas	Leftover meatballs from school.

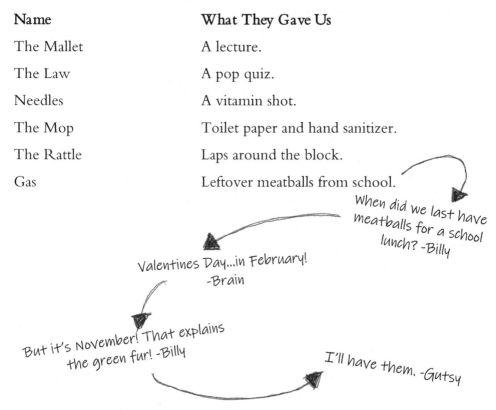

When did we last have meatballs for a school lunch? -Billy

Valentines Day...in February! -Brain

But it's November! That explains the green fur! -Billy

I'll have them. -Gutsy

And that's what happened....no candy....WORST HALLOWEEN EVER!

Before We Move On...A Page to Let Out Your Anger!

I don't feel better. -DD

Secret Smell of the Month

This is Gutsy and I'm not going to bother reading what's written under here as it's no secret that the smell of the month has been ruined! This whole idea of letting a girl join the gang has been a disaster! The scents of autumn? The subtle whiff of flowers? SHE'S BEEN SPRAYING PERFUME!
Our base smells of....our base smells of girl!

Gutsy, those smells were all me. I opened a window. -DD

REALLY?....Oh, then good job! -Gutsy

Password for the Month

ANITA BATH

After being in the gang for only four weeks I can honestly say that this applies to almost all of you! -Lou Lou

New Clubhouse Rules

	YES	NO
Any girl joining the gang will be given the name SHE WHO MUST BE BLAMED! -Gutsy	✓	✓
Anybody who calls me SHE WHO MUST BE BLAMED will have to go on a date with BIG SUE at our school. She's been in the 5th grade for three years and once wrestled a pig. She's a close friend of mine and she would love to hear that one of you wants to date her. -Lou Lou	✓	
Calling the girl SHE WHO MUST BE BLAMED is not allowed but only if she promises not to make the base all girly. -Gutsy	✓	
It's a deal....but I want a lock on the bathroom door. -Lou Lou	✓✓	
We all agree. -Gutsy	✓	✓

The rest of us didn't vote because we're all really confused and a little scared that we'll have to date big Sue if we voted the wrong way....That pig she wrestled; I heard it had to have therapy afterward! -DD

Grounded.... or why I'm not there!

Name: Gutsy

Status: Grounded

Reason: 1 + 3 + 1 = 7

or 1 (me) + 3 (D.I.E.) + 1 (enemy) = 7 days grounded.

So, I'm sitting in detention at school trying to write why I'm not there. But I have to pretend I'm doing math homework so this might look a little weird.

①   Water balloons
    + The D.I.E. Sisters
    + Me hiding in a tree

    = Too much temptation plus lots of fun

②   Water balloons
    + The D.I.E. Sisters
    + Me hiding in a tree
    + Me soaking all three of them

    = Hysterical plus priceless

③   Water balloons
    + The D.I.E. Sisters
    + Me hiding in a tree
    + Three very wet D.I.E. Sisters seeing me hiding

    = Not so much fun + suddenly scary

④   Water balloons
+ The D.I.E. Sisters
+ Needles watching me from her porch

= Negative fun plus infinite fear

⑤   Me hanging in a tree by my underpants
+ Needles sitting on her porch laughing at me
+ Needles inviting other enemies over
+ 20 minutes
+ All the enemies laughing at me
+ 3 hours
+ Tree branch finally breaks

= Painful walk home minus my dignity

⑥   Me picking underwear out of my butt
+ 30 minutes
+ Me finishing picking underwear out of my butt
+ The D.I.E. Sisters sending me an email
+ Me seeing photo of me hanging by underpants in tree
+ Me seeing they have sent photo to every kid in school
+ Embarrassment
+ Needles calling my Dad
+ Needles telling my Dad I broke her tree

= 7 days grounded plus 4 extra homework detentions

Minus dignity x 10

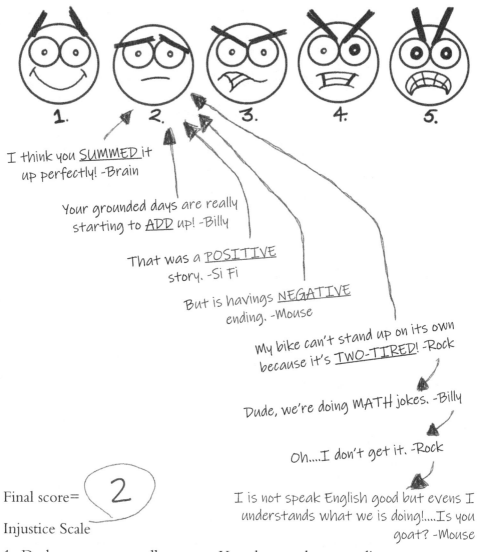

Free Nelson Update

by Rock withs Mouse

CHICKENBUTT! Oh, wait, I wrote that. -Rock

Days Grounded: 302

What did we learn about Nelson this month? We learned his Mom loves cats. She has a ton of them. And they aren't nice cats either! They are more likely to scratch your eyes out than curl up next to you!

After last month's mission, me and Mouse had this great idea to sneak up the drainpipe that Brain used to escape. Trouble was we couldn't get near it! If we so much as set foot in the backyard all we heard was hundreds of cats suddenly screeching. And if we set two feet in the backyard, one of them attacked us! We learned this when Mouse decided he was fast enough to make it to the house without them seeing him. He made it to the shed before he disappeared under a mountain of cats. Next thing we knew, Nelson's Mom came running out of the kitchen followed by The Mop, The Law, and Gas. I managed to grab Mouse and get out of there before they saw it was us but we didn't find anything out. Sorry guys. We failed.

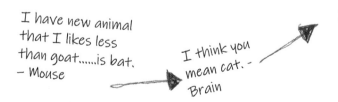

I have new animal that I likes less than goat......is bat. — Mouse

I think you mean cat. - Brain

I is being attacked by 50 cats....and you is worrying about how I is spelling? — Mouse

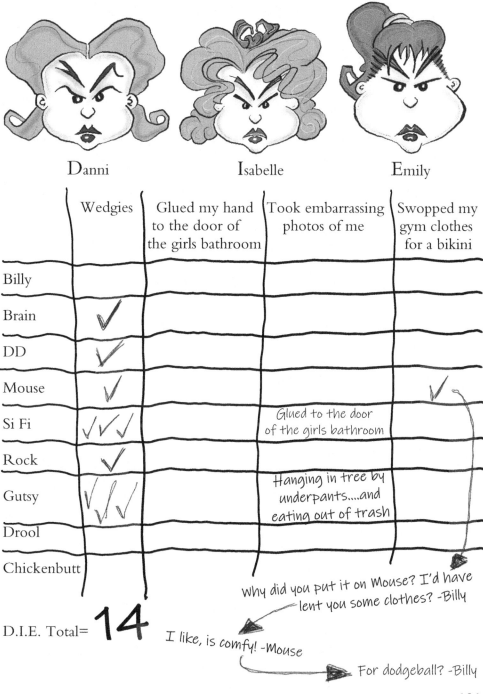

D.I.E. Update....continued by Billy

Hey! Us too! – Gutsy + Drool

I got them! That's right guys, score one for us! I got the D.I.E. Sisters! For the past week me, Gutsy, and Drool have been hiding out in the graveyard where they hang out, trying to see what the D.I.E. Sisters are planning. But we had no luck....so I decided it was time to play a little offense and give them a taste of their own medicine! Last week I got one of the 2nd graders to give D.I.E. a note saying they were needed in The Mallet's office.... IMMEDIATELY! Imagine their surprise when they got there only to find out they weren't needed after all! You should have seen their faces when they got to class nearly three minutes late! All of them looked a little bit annoyed and the teacher gave them a slightly disappointed look when they sat down. It was awesome! I got them!

That's it? That's what you call getting them? -DD

That is pretty lame Billy. They've been torturing us for months and you just mildly inconvenienced them. I don't think you can call that "getting them!" -Brain

Is that why they taped that 2nd grader to the wall yesterday? -Lou Lou

D.I.E. Update continued....

D.I.E. Update continued....told you it would be.... by Drool

While Billy's been off doing dumb stuff I've been hiding out watching D.I.E on my own. Gutsy's been grounded and Billy's too scared to set foot in a graveyard because he thinks they are all full of zombies! So, it was left to me to do some real work!

Guess what I found out? D.I.E. keeps a spare key to their base hidden in the graveyard....and I know where it is!

I saw Danni get it last week from behind an old gravestone. I know how to get into their base!

Now that's more like it! -DD

I still like my trick! -Billy

Let it go Billy....let it go..... -DD

Chickenbutt Bath Report by Brain

Before — The Problem (Chickenbutt) — After

The Solution: The Chickenbutt Bath Mobile 3.0
My Latest Invention

The Result: The EX-Chickenbutt Bath Mobile 3.0. FOR SALE. 1 owner.

Stuff We Didn't Get Grounded For....

- I rang the doorbell of my new neighbor, The Mallet, and ran away before he saw me! -Rock

- Oh wait, he did see me! -Rock

- He gave me a detention....and made me rake his yard. -Rock

- I'm going to stop writing now! -Rock

- Good luck naming anything we didn't get in trouble for this month! There's nothing! We can't get away with anything! The teachers are always watching us. We go to school, there they are....we go home, there they are! All we can do is come to this base or stay in our rooms. Everything else gets us in trouble! -Gutsy

  - You're still a little cranky from having no sugar aren't you? -Billy

  - A little, yes. -Gutsy

- Would candy help? I have some if you want it? -Lou Lou

- WHAT? REALLY? -Gutsy

- Just kidding....Chickenbutt! -Lou Lou

- I say we eat her. Maybe she tastes like caramel. -Gutsy

Final Thoughts by Billy

Great meeting guys! Good job!....I mean sure, we could spend our time thinking about all the bad stuff.

- So, we have no candy.
- So, we have no soda.
- So, we have no money.
- So, the teachers are our new neighbors.
- So, there's a girl in our gang.
- So, having no sugar is making us all cranky.

But guys, look on the bright side. Okay, don't look on the bright side, it's just as bad as this side. But December is a new month and I have a feeling that things are going to get better. Trust me guys, trust me!

Why is he so happy? Wait, he's been drinking soda hasn't he!? -DD

He found one under the couch this morning and he made me promise not to tell you all....he's so full of sugar right now, that's why he's so happy! -Drool

You are in so much trouble Belinda! -Si Fi

Well, this has been interesting....what a great gang I'm in! -Lou Lou

Assignments for Next Month by Billy

I feel so much better! -Drool

D.I.E. Update: We have a key! Drool and DD, this is your big moment! I want DD to keep watch while you two sneak in and take photos of everything. It's a very dangerous mission so take Chickenbutt just in case.

Project Free Nelson: Gutsy, Brain. Time for a new strategy. Security is just too tight at Nelson's house. I want you both to make a list of everyone who spends time there instead. Maybe it will give us some clues.

Drinks + Snacks: Lou Lou and Rock. Obviously, there's lots to do in this department so I want you to think of some fundraising ideas. We need some money!

Give Chickenbutt a Bath: Mouse. You came to this country to learn about our ways. Now it's time for you to teach us your ways. You can start by showing us the way to give Chickenbutt a bath.

Protect the Base: Chickenbutt, I know you'll be busy with the D.I.E. update so you can skip protecting the base this month. Feel free to skip farting too.

Grounded Gang Out!

Gutsy   Rock   DD   Drool

                    Mouse   (Chickenbutt)
                              Si Fi

        Billy   Lou Lou

FOR SALE: Little Brother
Needs work. Talks too much
and leaks at nightime.
Will sell for candy.
See Billy

December

CANDY!
Why did you leave us? WHY!? -DD

December Meeting by Billy

Letter from The President....to Santa!

Dear Santa,
This year I would like....
- A new bike.
- A new baseball mitt.
- All the enemies to move away from us.
- A room full of candy.

Thank-you,
Billy

P.S. Oh yeah, give me some of that world peace stuff and a bit of that goodwill to all men thingy. Oh, and some new video games.

P.P.S When you are deciding how good I've been all year I know it doesn't look good that I'm in a gang that keeps getting grounded. But I promise you we are all good kids. The ones you should really be annoyed at are D.I.E. and the teachers. I'd love to see the list of things they've done wrong this year....

If you have that list could I get a copy of it to blackmail them with?

If that's a "no", can I just get a new flat screen TV instead?

December Meeting Continued.... by Billy

Okay guys, as your President you know I like to try to be positive. Like all great leaders, I am your role model and I think of it as my job to keep all of you feeling happy; especially through the hard times. But I'll be honest, it's been tough this month. No Nelson, no money, no sugar. Don't even get me started on what it's like to live by the enemies! Just getting to base to write up this meeting was nearly impossible. The Hammer stopped me and questioned me for 30 minutes about who glued his mailbox shut. Then, Needles gave me a 20 minute lecture on how to check your own head for lice. Not to mention the fact that I had to see The Law doing yoga on her front lawn. When she bent over, I swear, the sky went dark for a few seconds.

And then, to top it all, I walk into the base yesterday and what do I find? THIS! We have to draw a line somewhere guys and this is it! This can't be allowed to happen!

Me! -DD

SEE NEXT PAGE....I warn you though, it's bad....it's really, really bad! -Billy

Our Base

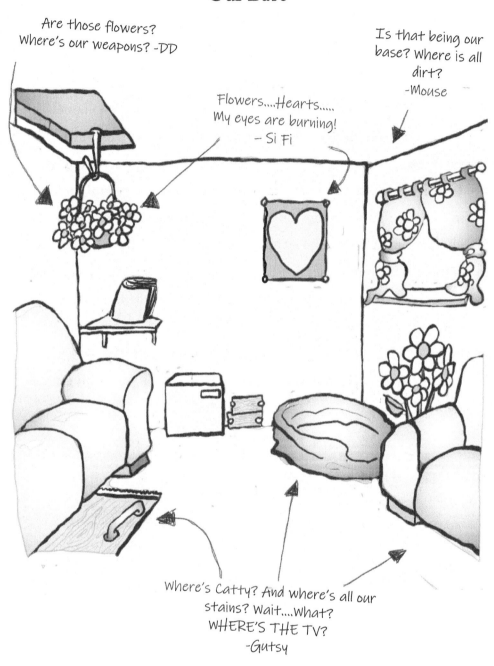

Okay guys. What happened to our base is awful, but I think it's only fair that we give the person who did it a chance to explain their actions.

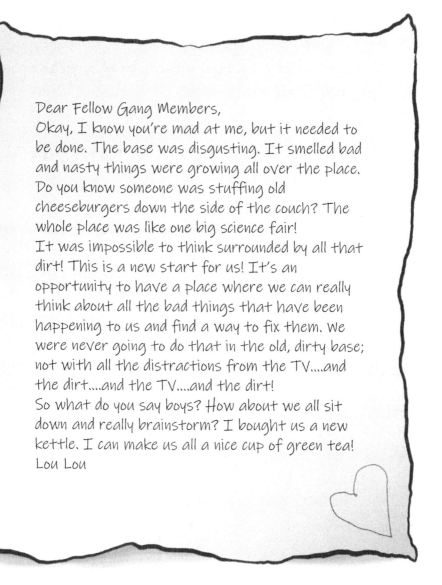

Dear Fellow Gang Members,
Okay, I know you're mad at me, but it needed to be done. The base was disgusting. It smelled bad and nasty things were growing all over the place. Do you know someone was stuffing old cheeseburgers down the side of the couch? The whole place was like one big science fair!
It was impossible to think surrounded by all that dirt! This is a new start for us! It's an opportunity to have a place where we can really think about all the bad things that have been happening to us and find a way to fix them. We were never going to do that in the old, dirty base; not with all the distractions from the TV....and the dirt....and the TV....and the dirt!
So what do you say boys? How about we all sit down and really brainstorm? I bought us a new kettle. I can make us all a nice cup of green tea!
Lou Lou

So, now that we've heard from Lou Lou, why don't we move ahead with the meeting.

First thing I'd like to do is cancel next month's vote to decide if we keep Lou Lou in the gang.

Let's have it now instead! I don't care if she shows everyone that photo. Nobody touches our TV!

Should We Keep Lou Lou in the Gang?

	YES	NO
Billy		✓
Brain		✓
Double Dare		✓
Mouse		✓
Si FI		✓
Rock		✓
Gusty		✓
Drool		✓
Chickenbutt		

Lou Lou, anything you'd like to say before you leave?

Okay, I know when I'm not wanted. I'll go quietly. Don't worry, I won't start crying or anything. I get it.

Oh, before I go, I was hoping to tell you this over tea but, I wanted to mention that my Dad got a new job. He's now the manager of the biggest candy factory in the country. Ever since he started there my house is full of free samples. I've got more candy than I know what to do with! There's certainly enough to keep the base filled with candy forever.

I brought in a big, huge bag so you could try some for yourselves. But, I guess that's of no interest to any of you anymore....

I'll just take my candy and leave.

Farewell Grounded Gang,

Lou Lou

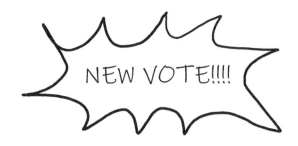

Should We Keep Lou Lou in the Gang?

	YES	NO
Billy	✓	
Brain	✓	
Double Dare	✓	
Mouse	✓	
Si FI	✓	
Rock	✓	
Gusty	✓	
Drool	✓	
Chickenbutt		

Is it too late for some of that green tea? It sounds wonderful! Maybe we could enjoy it with some of that candy you mentioned?
-Gutsy

Official Break in the Meeting

There will now be an official half
hour break while we enjoy some
tea and candy in our lovely
new base! -Billy

Stuff for December

Roll Call

Special Halloween Report

Secret Smell of the Month

Password for the Month

New Clubhouse Rules

Grounded……or Why I'm Not There

Scale of Injustice

Free Nelson Update

D.I.E. Update

Chickenbutt Bath Report

Stuff We Didn't Get Grounded for this Month

Final Thoughts

Assignments for Next Month

Ooooh this all looks good. I'm excited for this meeting. -DD

Are you all feeling a little happier now?! -Lou Lou

Rollcall

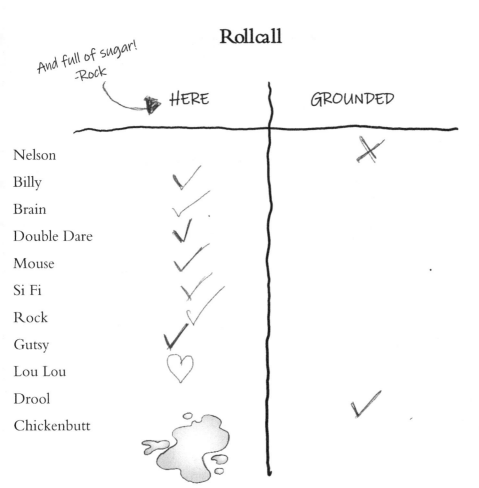

And full of sugar! —Rock

	HERE	GROUNDED
Nelson		X
Billy	✓	
Brain	✓	
Double Dare	✓	
Mouse	✓	
Si Fi	✓	
Rock	✓	
Gutsy	✓	
Lou Lou	♡	
Drool		✓
Chickenbutt	(puddle)	

Secret Smell of the month......by Lou Lou

Want....to say something bad about smell, but don't...want to lose....candy. - Gutsy

Well, obviously, I had to choose something in keeping with our new wonderful base. That's why I made my own potpourri!!! Of course I don't expect you to know what potpourri is but, it was invented by the French in the 17th century and originally made using summer flowers rubbed in a sea salt. Today you are more likely to find potpourri that contains cedar, cinnamon, jasmine, lavender, lemon, mint, orange or even roses! For this month's smell I chose a potpourri made with extra fennel and juniper to energize us all. Isn't it yummy?!

How does a pot with a jumper and a funnel in it smell so bad? She really needs to learn how to spell! - Rock

Is this what Barbie's farts smell like? -Si Fi

Password for the Month

This months password will be:

SID DOWN

I think I know his brother? Stan Dup! - DD

151

New Clubhouse Rules by Lou Lou

Dear Gang,

This month I asked Billy if I could be in charge of the new clubhouse rules. He said no. I gave him some candy. He said yes. You boys are so easy. Anyway, now that you have a girl in the gang I've decided that you all need to be a little more civilized. That's why I'm introducing a few new rules for the bathroom at our base.

1. The toilet will no longer be known as Mr. Stinky or The Pooper.
2. What you do in the bathroom will **ONLY** be known as using the bathroom. It will no longer be known as "making plip-plop", "blowing my own horn", or "closing the pool".
3. The toilet seat will be put up when you go pee. *The toilet seat goes up? - Rock*
4. The score chart, Mr. Yellow vs. Mrs. Brown, will no longer be used.
5. As soon as we get some money the gang will buy some soft toilet paper. Newspaper, old candy wrappers, and letters from school will no longer be used.
6. If you sprinkle when you tinkle please be sweet and wipe the seat.

7. And if by mistake, you stand too soon, please try not to flood the room! - Drool

Continued....

Just in case you still have the urge to talk about what you plan to do in the bathroom I have created the following codes for you to use instead. Why boys insist on telling each other everything about what you plan to do in the toilet I'll never know! At least, this way, I won't have to hear about it!

CODE	WHAT IT MEANS
Number 1	I'm going to go pee.
Number 2	I'm going to go poop.
Number 3	I'm going 1 or 2 while eating a sandwich.
Number 4	I'm going 1 or 2 with the door open so I can see the TV.
Number 5	I'm about to do something in there that may require you all to stop breathing for 1-2 hours.

Do you all agree to all these new rules and promise not to change your mind later when the sugar wears off?

Yes   No

Don't....want....to....vote....yes....but....love candy... -Gutsy

Do all new toilets rules being true for trash can too?
-Mouse

Grounded.... or why I'm not there!

Name: Drool

Status: Grounded

Reason: My ball went to see the nurse.

Drool Grounding.... The Scale of Injustice

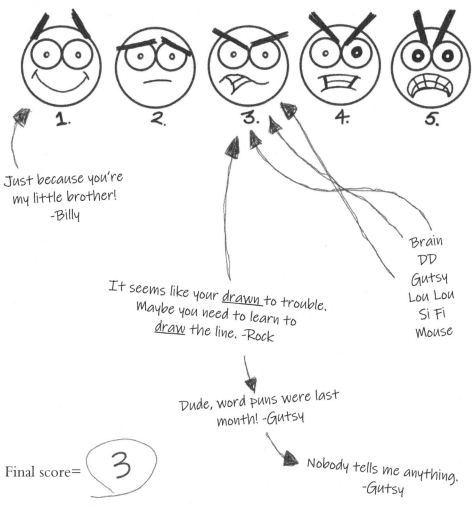

Injustice Scale

1- Dude, you were totally wrong. You deserve the grounding.

2- Alright, it was a mistake. But, dude, you were still wrong.

3- Well, that wasn't cool, was it? They didn't have to ground you for that.

4- Whoa, that's totally not right. You don't deserve to be grounded for that.

5- WHAT!? That's not fair. Stay where you are, we're coming to get you.

Free Nelson Update

by Brain with Gutsy

Days Grounded: 333

Assignment: List all the people coming and going at Nelson's house.

<u>Monday</u>

10am   Delivery person arrives with 3 large cases of cat food.
11am   The Rattle arrives. Bangs head on way into house but doesn't seem to notice.
1pm   Two cats arrive at the front door. One leaves carrying envelope in mouth.
3pm   The Hammer arrives carrying shovel. He looks tired.
5pm   Pizza delivery. Nelson's Mom pays for 6 pizzas.
5:05pm   Pizza delivery guy leaves. Gutsy decides he is so hungry that he chases after him and asks to smell his delivery bag.
5:10pm   Pizza delivery guy runs away from hungry boy who is trying to lick old pizza cheese off his car seat.
5:15pm   Pizza delivery guy calls police. We leave.

<u>Tuesday</u>

10am   Delivery person arrives with 3 more large cases of cat food.
11am   The Law arrives carrying a bag of tools. She looks tired and is wearing her pajamas.
12pm   4 cats arrive. 2 cats leave.
1pm   Chinese food delivery guy arrives. Nelson's Mom pays.
1:05pm Chinese food delivery guy leaves, chased by Gutsy asking to smell his bag.
1:15pm Chinese food delivery guy calls the police. We hide in the bushes.
2pm   Needles arrives just as The Law leaves. They ignore each other. The Law is sweaty and looks like she has been exercising. She has her eyes closed the whole time.
4pm   The D.I.E. Sisters arrive carrying several shopping bags and a hammer (the tool, not the teacher).
4:05pm Gutsy farts.
4:05pm and 2 seconds. I leave.

Wednesday

5am — I don't know! I was in bed so couldn't tell you!

10am — Delivery person arrives with 3 more large cases of cat food.

11am — The Rattle arrives wearing a baseball helmet with a flashlight taped to it.

11:05am — 4 cats arrive, 1 leaves carrying small box tied to collar.

11:30am — Needles and The Mop arrive carrying several large pieces of wood. Needles drops one piece of wood on The Mop's foot but he doesn't seem to notice.

12pm — Sandwich delivery guy arrives. Nelson's Mom pays for 10 large sandwiches.

12:05pm — Gutsy holds onto sandwich delivery guys leg begging for food. Sandwich delivery guy defends himself with a tuna hero before running away.

12:06pm — Gutsy spends 45 happy minutes eating bits of tuna out of his hair.

1pm — The Law arrives carrying a pickaxe.

1:30pm — 3 more cats arrive.

4pm — D.I.E. Sisters arrive.

4:45pm — I think I have just seen a miracle! The D.I.E. Sisters left and one was smiling! She must have been doing something really, really bad.

Thursday

10am   Delivery person arrives with 3 more large cases of cat food.
11am   The Hammer arrives carrying axe. He looks sleepy.
12pm   Mexican food delivery arrives. I sit on Gutsy until they leave.
2:30pm   Gutsy coughs as 2 cats are arriving. This seems to upset them even though they are a long way away.
2:32pm   6 cats leave. They seem to be searching for something.
2:35pm   9 more cats join them. They seem to be meowing a lot.
2:37pm   How clever. They are circling something. It must be a bird or a small animal. I didn't know cats could work in teams like that!
2:38pm   IT'S US! They cats are circling our hiding place! They are definitely working together! This is fascinating!
2:39pm   Not quite so fascinating anymore. Cats look angry.
2:40pm   Cats seem to be forming some sort of attack group. I'm starting to get worried.
2:41pm   Cats getting very close now. I tell Gutsy that as long as we stick together we'll be fine.
2:42pm   Gutsy runs away and leaves me on my own!
2:43pm   Cats right by me now....I think they see me. No time. Have to leave before it's too late.
2:44pm   It's too late.

Friday

9am   At home. You have to be kidding me if you think I'm going back to Nelson's anytime soon.

10am Going to Gutsy's house to ask him why I'm covered in cat scratches and he isn't!

What we learned:

- Nelson's Mom really likes cats.

- She also really likes to order takeout food.

- The teachers are at Nelson's house A LOT!

- If you want Gutsy to sit in one place, for a long time, pack a lunch.

- Don't mess with cats.

- Something weird is happening at Nelson's house!

Do you think she'd adopt me? -Gutsy

Interesting.... -Lou Lou

D.I.E. Update

	Wedgies	Made me smell Emily's sneaker	Took embarrassing photos of me	Made me eat a worm
Billy				
Brain	✓			✓
DD	✓ ✓	while she was wearing it		
Mouse	✓	✓		✓
Si Fi	✓	✓		
Rock	✓			
Gutsy	✓		Eating out of trash	It was soooo good!
Drool		✓		
Chickenbutt				
Lou Lou				

D.I.E. Total = 15

D.I.E Update....continued....

Breaking into D.I.E's base by DD
with Drool & Chickenbutt

Okay, it didn't go quite to plan! At first, everything was fine. We waited for D.I.E. to leave then, I went to get the spare key while Drool got his camera ready to take lots of pictures. Then we left Chickenbutt to guard the front door. When I say we left him on guard I mean we dragged the big sleeping ball of fur as close to door as we could without making him fart....which was about 3 steps!

Before we knew it, we were inside. We were inside D.I.E.'s secret base! It was so cool. Also, smelly. And the lights didn't work....so, it was just kinda dark and smelly. You'd think a girls base would be nicer? Anyway, we kept going, searching for anything we could use against D.I.E. It was difficult without a flashlight but,

Are you kidding me! -Lou Lou

slowly we began finding things. First, we found something wet and sticky. Upon closer inspection it turned out to be a wet stick. The next thing we

found was dusty and boney. Upon closer inspection it was a dusty bone. Then, we found something slimy and fishy. We left that alone.

Then, we saw it. Sitting on an old table was a book with thick black letters on it's front.

D.I.E. Diary.

This was what we'd been looking for! All I could think of was how much power we'd have if we had the diary of the D.I.E. Sisters! If we knew all their secrets, they'd never dare give us wedgies ever again! Both of us rushed over to the table but as soon we took a step we heard it.

'Gggrrrrrrrrrr'

We looked at each other for a second before taking another step.

'Ggggggggggrrrrrrrrrrrrrrrrrr'

Now we definitely knew that something wasn't right.

'Ggggggggggggggrrrrrrrrrrrrrrrrrrrrrrrrrrr'

We wanted to run but the book was right there, tempting us.

'Ggggggggggggggggggggggggggggrrrrrrrrrrrrrrrrrrrrrrrrrrrrrrrr'

We ran to grab the book but before we got close, it was on us. Its huge front legs, like two massive trees, pinning us to the floor. Bright flashes started to surround us as the camera fell from Drool's pocket and began going crazy. Blinded, I tried to push the huge animal off me but could only feel the drool from its huge fangs, dripping onto my face. We were finished. The D.I.E. Sisters were too smart. They had some sort of huge beast guarding their base, and it was going to eat us. BANG!

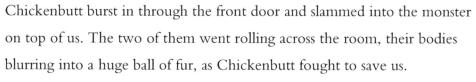

Chickenbutt burst in through the front door and slammed into the monster on top of us. The two of them went rolling across the room, their bodies blurring into a huge ball of fur, as Chickenbutt fought to save us.

For a second we lay there, frozen in surprise, as the flashing camera filled the room with pictures of Chickenbutt and the beast battling.

Then a loud bark reminded us we needed to get out of there. We scrambled to our feet just as the camera flashed again, leaving us both blinded. Then, I felt something brush against my fingers. It was the book! But before I could grab it, Chickenbutt and the beast banged hard into the table, sending the book flying. Its pages started to fall around us like snow. Fear took over us again and we both ran for the door, grabbing all the pages we could, as Drool snatched up the camera. Once outside we kept running until we got back to our base. Unfortunately, most of the pages we managed to grab were blank. Except for one.

Chickenbutt came trotting in 10 minutes later, acting as if nothing had happened. Both of us were so grateful to him for saving us that we gave him a special treat; 8 hot dogs. Looking back, this was a bad idea as it made his farts stronger than anything Lou Lou's pot of poury could ever cover.

Overall, I don't know if the mission was a success. But I'll tell you this, you can count us out of ever going back there again; not with the beast they've got guarding their base!

D.I.E Update Evidence #1: A page from D.I.E's Diary

Thursday

The weird kid with the mask and the glove on his head bumped into me today in the hallway. I gave him a wedgie and he called me something I didn't understand. So I gave him another wedgie. He had a picture of unicorns on his underpants. -Emily

Friday

We're all tired and miserable again this morning. None of us has the energy to give anyone a wedgie. Don't know whats wrong with us. We all took a nap today too, but it didn't help. We're going to go out and get one of The Grounded Gang to make ourselves feel better. -Danni

Saturday

I love Billy. He is so cute and dre~~ ~~. I wish that he would

Billy and D.I.E sitting in a tree. K.I.S.S.I....No, I can't do it. Just thinking about it makes me want to throw up! -Drool

What???? -Billy

Chickenbutt....has a girlfriend! -Gutsy

Ha! Is not true! Is mermaids on my underpants! They is wrong....oh waits....mermaids is embarrassings too. -Mouse

D.I.E Update Evidence #2: by Billy

Thought you might like to see this. The camera that Drool used was mine. And when he dropped it, the camera went crazy and took lots of photos. He told me it was broken and then he threw it in the trash. But I took it out and guess what? It still worked! Most of the photos it took were useless but, it did manage to take one very interesting picture....

The Beast of D.I.E.'s Base

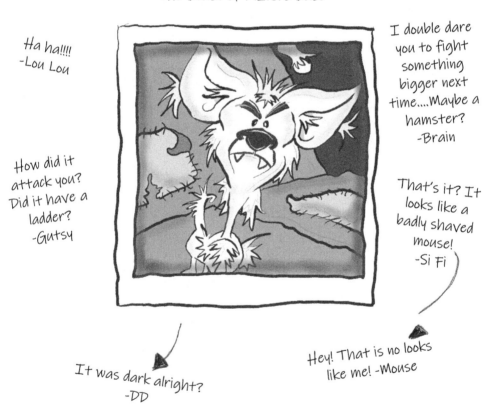

Ha ha!!!!
-Lou Lou

I double dare you to fight something bigger next time....Maybe a hamster?
-Brain

How did it attack you? Did it have a ladder?
-Gutsy

That's it? It looks like a badly shaved mouse!
-Si Fi

It was dark alright?
-DD

Hey! That is no looks like me! -Mouse

Chickenbutt Bath Report *by Mouse*

Is photo of me before bath and then is photo of me after bath. Is also photo of Chickenbutt watching me taking bath. I is not knowing why you is thinking me taking baths is important assignment but I haves to say I no minds this. I is like bath. -Mouse

Err, Mouse, you know you were supposed to give Chickenbutt a bath, not take one yourself? -Billy

Really...? Oh, is my bad. Is must be me not understanding because me is still learnings English. Is not because me is scared of giving Chickenbutts a bath so me is pretends that me don'ts understands....I is promising.... -Mouse

Evil genius! -Brain

Drinks and Snacks Fundraising Report by Lou Lou with Rock

We need money. But when Rock and I sat down to make a list of fundraising ideas it quickly became obvious that only ONE of us had any intelligence at all. That's why I decided we should make 2 separate lists. I think you'll find that only ONE of them is worth looking at!

Lou Lou's List

Lemonade stand ⟶ Oooh, I'm allergic to lemons - DD

Paper route ⟶ Doesn't that require getting up early? - SiFi

Sell cupcakes ⟶ Cooking, what are we girls???? - Gutsy

Mow lawns ⟶ Sounds sweaty - Drool

Yard clean up ⟶ Even more sweaty - Billy

Dog grooming ⟶ We can't even manage the dog we have! -Brain

Gentlemen. I give you the best way for us to make money. -Rock ⟶

I talked to Brain and he's building us a robot! -Rock

Genius! -Billy

Brilliant! -DD

Far Out! -Si Fi

I is like very much! -Mouse

Cool! -Drool

Amazing! -Si Fi

THIS? I give you a whole list of great ideas and you choose making a robot to fight another robot? Are you all really that lazy? -Lou Lou

You really need to relax. Have you had some candy? -Rock

Stuff We Didn't Get Grounded For....

- Licking The Hammers car....it's a long story. -Gutsy

- I don't want to talk about it! -Gutsy

- I was hungry alright!? -Gutsy

- So, he'd left a box of candy bars on his front seat. -Gutsy

- And I could see them getting all melted and gooey. -Gutsy

- They looked so good that I could almost taste them! -Gutsy

- It was like they were hypnotizing me. -Gutsy

- Next thing I know I'm licking The Hammers car window. -Gutsy

- ....trying to get my mouth closer to the candy. -Gutsy

- That's when Dad walked by. -Gutsy

- Now I have to see a therapist once a week. -Gutsy

- But I didn't get grounded! -Gutsy

Final Thoughts by Billy

Good job everyone. This month has been the best meeting for a while. Sure, some would say it's just because we got sugar again but, I like to think it's much more than that. We didn't just get sugar, we got an endless supply of sugar. It's totally different.

We're also starting to get somewhere with working out why we keep getting grounded. Okay, so we didn't really find out anything at D.I.E.'s base and the teachers still hate us. Oh, and there's an army of cats that seem to hate us too.…Did I mention we got an endless supply of sugar?

Except that D.I.E loves Billy! -Drool

Oh, Lou Lou asked me to remind you all to keep the base clean and not mess up all her hard work.

Because it would be really bad if the base got all dirty again.

Now, if it were to get dirty again by accident it would just be one of those things. And you can't really get mad at an accident.…can you?!

Accidents happen all the time.

Me is getting message. You is our leader and you is wanting that our base is being super clean and no accidents. You is able to counts on me. -Mouse

Oh, good grief! -Billy

Assignments for Next Month by Billy

Lou Lou asked if she could decide the assignments this month. She said something about thinking she was onto something and wanting us to follow the clues she was seeing. I don't know, I wasn't really listening.

<u>D.I.E. Update</u>- Mouse, Drool, Si Fi. Go back and get the rest of that diary. Lou Lou thinks that we really need it. Take Chickenbutt. If you are worried about the beast just give it some cheese and put it in your pocket. I hear mice like that.

<u>Free Nelson Update</u>- Gutsy, DD. Follow one of those cats when it leaves Nelson's house and see where it goes. Lou Lou thinks that cats are the key to all of this. Not a clue why.

<u>Chickenbutt Bath Update</u> – Lou Lou. Well, you picked it! Don't worry, I'm sure he'll be nice!

<u>Drinks and Snacks/Fundraising</u>- Brain. Build us a robot and win us some money. Rock, you get to carry stuff around for Brain.

<u>Protect the Base-</u> Chickenbutt. Lou Lou says you showed that you are perfect for this job. I want to add that you should do lots of farting. That pot of purry stinks

Grounded Gang Out!

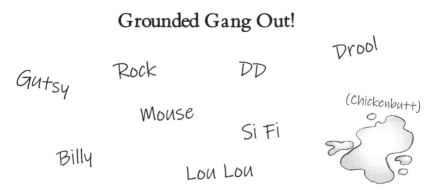

January

What is this?
-Si Fi

January Meeting by Billy

Letter from The President:

Happy New Year! Well, it would be if we weren't all grounded! This month has been the worst so far. Four of us grounded! Lou Lou says that it's all connected, and that all the clues are starting to make sense. She tried to explain it but I was too busy playing video games so she got mad. I think she's cranky because of all the construction noise outside her house keeping her awake. Girls!

But, there's good news too. Because our fundraising didn't work out quite as well as we would have hoped, I have started a new money maker for the gang….advertising! That's right, kids at school will actually pay us to advertise stuff that they want to sell…to us. It's easy money! I got the idea when this kid in my class said he'd invented a special cream that stopped wedgies hurting. I said I'd put an ad in our meeting book if he wanted………for a dollar! It's that easy! No more worrying about money. We just put some ads in the book every month and then sit back and watch the dollars roll in!

Oh, by the way, don't buy that cream. It tastes awful.

You're not supposed to eat it! You're supposed to rub it on your………… what! - Brain

Chickenbutt! -Gutsy

Exactly! -Brain

Grounded Gang Central

Stuff for January

Roll Call

Secret Smell of the Month

Password for the Month

New Clubhouse Rules

Grounded.......or Why I'm Not There

Scale of Injustice

Free Nelson Update

D.I.E. Update

Chickenbutt Bath Report

Stuff We Didn't Get Grounded For This Month

What We Learned This Month

Final Thoughts

Assignments for Next Month

Rollcall

	HERE	GROUNDED
Nelson		✗
Billy	✓	
Brain		✓
Double Dare		✓
Mouse		✓
Si Fi	✓	
Rock		✓
Gutsy	✓	
Lou Lou	♡	
Drool	✓	
Chickenbutt	💧	

Secret Smell of the Month.....by Si Fi

I thought I'd bring in something special for us. It's a magic pink moon rock that The Mop sold me. He said it was discovered by the astronauts on the very first moon landing! Its so powerful that NASA ordered them to leave it behind but one of the astronauts managed to smuggle one back in his underpants. And The Mop sold me it for only $20! He says it has a magic ability to absorb all bad smells .....forever! And I got it for our base! We'll never need to worry about smells again!

Dude that's a urinal cake. They use them in the boys bathrooms at school. - DD

Password for the Month

This months password will be:

LOU KOUT

In this country you put cakes in your toilets? - Mouse

BEHIND YOU!

Did someone say there was cake?- Gutsy

Clubhouse Rules

	YES	NO
The toilet seat must go up when you use the toilet! -Lou Lou		✓
The toilet seat stays down! -Billy		✓
Up! -Lou Lou		✓
Down! -Billy		✓
UP! -Lou Lou		✓
Tell us where you hid the TV and we'll put it up! – Billy	✓✓✓✓✓	
Oh alright....deal! -Lou Lou	✓	
YES!!!! -Billy	✓✓✓✓✓	

Grounded.... or Why I'm Not There by Brain with Rock

Name: Brain and Rock
Status: Grounded
Reason: We blew up the lockers.

That's it! I don't want to be paired up with Rock on anymore assignments! Two weeks I'm grounded for....TWO WEEKS! No experiments, no nothing. Just school and sitting in my bedroom listening to the work crew banging away outside my window. I'm going to die of boredom....all because of Rock!

I didn't do it! -Rock

Our assignment was so simple too. Win Robot Wars and get money. And I was ready. The robot I'd built was unbeatable! Lazers for eyes, spiked hammers for hands, a giant axe for a head, this thing could have destroyed a tank! I called it 2DIE4. But, on the day of the wars, I hit a problem. We had to be at the stadium 2 hours before the war started, but I didn't have time to go home after school to get 2DIE4. The only thing I could do was bring it to school with me. So, I asked Rock to help me sneak it into my locker. That way we had plenty of time to get 2DIE4 to the stadium before the end of the day. Simple.

I'm telling you it was not my fault! -Rock

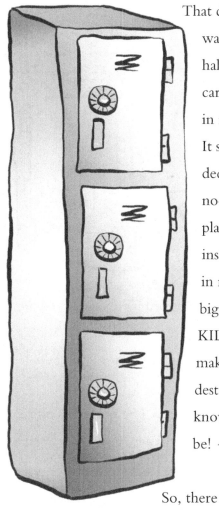

That day we got to school early, before anyone was around. Only, The Mop was in the hallway, so I distracted him while Rock carried 2DIE4 into the building and put him in my locker. Simple, or so I thought.

It seemed that one us, let's call him ROCK, decided that while I was making sure that no-one saw us, he would spend his time playing with the buttons on our robot. So, instead of hiding a nice quiet sleeping robot in my locker he'd put one in there with a big red flashing light that said, "READY TO KILL". All it needed was for someone to make the slightest noise and 2DIE4 would destroy everything in it's path. And we all know how quiet a school full of children can be!

I didn't play with any buttons!!! - Rock

So, there we were in class when The Hammer came over the speaker and said it was time for the Pledge of Allegiance. Every one stood up....and that was when....

BANG!....Every kid in school heard 2DIE4 blow the door off my locker with it's laser eyes.

CRASH!....Using it's hammer hands, it destroyed four more lockers before heading for the teachers' lounge.

SMASH!....Using the axe on it's head he sliced the couch in half.

I grabbed Rock and ran down the hallway just in time to see 2DIE4 begin its attack on the staff fridge. Confiscated snacks were flying everywhere and a can of soda flew past my head and destroyed the school trophy cabinet. That was when I remembered 2DIE4's remote control in my school bag! I shouted for Rock to go get it and ducked under a storm of cheese crackers as I tried to get closer. Minutes later, Rock slid me the remote control just as 2DIE4 raised it's axe and took aim at the Mr. Coffee machine. I hit the off switch, but it was too late. With a final swing 2DIE4's axe wedged itself into the coffee pot as it's red eyes slowly faded to black.

Then I felt it. The hand of The Law dragging me to The Hammers office. Needles and Rock were right behind and before I knew it, we were being asked to explain why the teachers' lounge had just been destroyed by a robot killing machine.

I tried to tell them that it wasn't anything to do with us when The Hammer pressed play on the security camera. It turns out it's kind of hard to pretend your innocent when they have video of a certain someone, let's call him Rock, running down the hallway yelling, "BRAIN, I'VE GOT IT! I HAVE THE REMOTE CONTROL FOR THE ROBOT YOU BUILT THAT JUST DESTROYED THE TEACHERS LOUNGE!"

Yeah, looking back that was kinda silly. -Rock

The only thing that could have possibly made it worse was the teachers showing the video to my parents.

"Both your parents will be getting a copy of this…….along with a bill for a new teacher's lounge!" said The Law.

Oh yeah, that was the other thing that could have made it worse….losing your allowance for the next six months, to pay for a new teacher's lounge! No more missions with Rock………..EVER!

Hurtful!!!! -Rock

Brain and Rock Grounding.... The Scale of Injustice

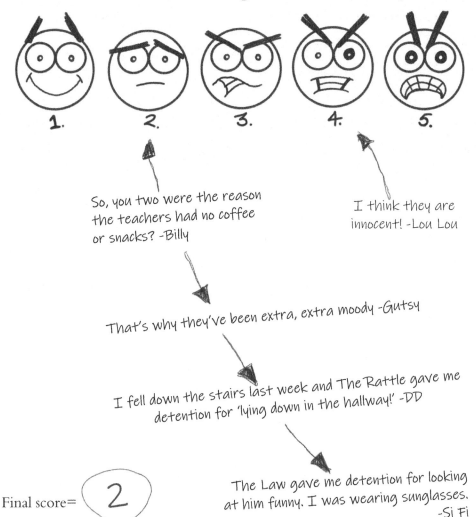

So, you two were the reason the teachers had no coffee or snacks? -Billy

I think they are innocent! -Lou Lou

That's why they've been extra, extra moody -Gutsy

I fell down the stairs last week and The Rattle gave me detention for 'lying down in the hallway!' -DD

The Law gave me detention for looking at him funny. I was wearing sunglasses. -Si Fi

Final score = 2

Injustice Scale

1- Dude, you were totally wrong. You deserve the grounding.
2- Alright, it was a mistake. But, dude, you were still wrong.
3- Well, that wasn't cool, was it? They didn't have to ground you for that.
4- Whoa, that's totally not right. You don't deserve to be grounded for that.
5- WHAT!? That's not fair. Stay where you are, we're coming to get you.

Grounded.... or Why I'm Not There by Mouse with DD

Name: Mouse and DD
Status: Grounded
Reason: Our robot was too hairy.

So, we is standing there after seeing robot go crazy. We is seeing Brains and Rocks being taken to The Mallets office. I know this is very bads. Gang is needings money. We has candy but we needs money for soda. Me is liking soda very much. So, I says to Double Dares, "Lets gets the robot and you and me take it to Robot Wars." I can sees Double Dares thinks this is good ideas two so we both sneaks up to get robot while no-one is seeing. But befores we know it, The Mop is theres. *Interesting.... -Lou Lou* "Let's lock you up safely this time," he is saying. Then he is laughing and picking ups robot.

I think this is funny things to say as he no locks it up the first time but before I has thinkings time Double Dares pulls me away and tells me to be quiets. We go into bathrooms where Double Dares tells me he has ideas. He says if we cannot take Brains robot we should make new one.

Then he asks me if me knows how to makes a fighting robots. I say no buts I have seen two goats wrestling before. Is like big famous sports in my country. Then he say that I have just given him worlds best ideas and that I should meet him after school is over. Worlds best ideas is toilets paper, so I knows he is lyings but I meet hims anyways.

After school we is going straight to base. When we gets there, Double Dares is tellings me to waits outside as he has surprise for me. All I is thinking is 'Please don't be goats, please don't be goats.' So, when Double Dares is coming out with no goat I is very happy. Instead, he is bringing out Chickenbutt wrapped in shiny silver paper. "I made a robot," he says. I no know very much about robots but I no think Chickenbutt looks like robots. I want to tells Double Dares is bad ideas but he is very prouds of what he has done. He tells me that he has covered Chickenbutt in something called tin foil and how he will beat all other robots. I no so sure.

When we gets to robot wars, peoples is lookings funny at us. Other peoples have robots that look likes robots. We have big hairy dog that is wrapped up like sandwich.

So, is big surprise when man at desk says is okay for Chickenbutt to go in arena! Double Dares say is because Chickenbutt looks like a great robot. I thinks is because man is too busy picking his nose to see we have big silver dog, not robot.

Inside, man with clipboard gives us funny look and tell us to put Chickenbutt, (he call him "whatever that thing is"), in cage number 15. Then lights go out. Then lights go on again. Doors to cages open. Robots is rushing out and is beginnings to smashing and crashing each others. Is very noisy and bits of broken robots is flying all around our heads. This is very dangerous place and me is think that maybe we makes a mistake putting Chickenbutt in there. Then, I think that I cannot see Chickenbutt! Double Dares is looking over into cage and groaning. He is seeing that Chickenbutt is asleep! By nows lots of robots is broken and smash on floor and only one robot in arena is still moving. Is big green robot called 'Death Machine'. Death Machine has long fingers like knife and big hammer on back that he use to make all other robots very flat like pancake. When all other robots are dead, Death Machine see Chickenbutt asleep in cage. He drive over and raise big hammer up, ready to smash. Then Chickenbutt open one eye. Before Death Machine know what is happening Chickenbutt is jumping up and down ontop of him. He is waving knife fingers in air but Chickenbutt is like ninja and everytime he land on Death Machine he is smashing his own hammer on top of him. Death Machine is not looking so big now and sparks is coming out of his butt. Soon Death Machine is flat like all other robots. Chickenbutt is stopping jumping and is looking at him. Then he is lie down and go back to sleep. Then we realize. WE HAS WON ROBOT WARS! We is so happy we runs into arena and is jumping ups and downs in fronts of all the peoples watchings. Peoples looks confused but is all clappings like we is big heros. Then man with clipboard come over and get out big check with 250 dollars written on it.

> Really? Robots don't have butts.
> -Brain

> Dude, it had a butt. You could tell it was a butt because it was all rusty.
> -DD

189

I is very excited and is thinking of all the soda we can buy with money. Me don't knows if me ever tells you this but me loves soda! Man with clipboard is ready to give us money when we hears it, a noise like mouse playing trumpet. Chickenbutt is farting.

Man look at Chickenbutt then he look at us. "Robots don't fart.... that's not a robot is it?" he says. We wants to say yes is robot but Chickenbutt is fart again, but louder this time like cow jumping in swimming pool full of mud. This fart is so louds that all peoples watchings can hears it. Then whole arena starts to smell like rotten egg.

People in crowds is startings booings and throwing things at us. Then man with clipboard tell us to leave. We pick-ups Chickenbutts and go but outsides I feels tap on shoulder. Is The Mop. He says he see what is happening and he is telling our parents....and he is doing just that. Now we is grounded for two weeks. Oh, and we need more tin foil. We is out.

Interesting! -Lou Lou

I sold another ad! -Billy

DATE NEEDED

Boy needed to accompany girl to family wedding. Personally I find the whole thing ridiculous but my parents seem to thing I need to "get my head out of books and do things that normal girls my age do." This is, of course, completely illogical so I've decided to teach them a lesson and bring a "bad-boy." You all seem to keep getting in trouble so if one of you accompanies me I am willing to pay you $5 and an additional $1 if you don't annoy me too much. No hand-holding, no staring into my eyes, and DEFINITELY NO KISSING! Oh, and don't fall in love with me. I am not interested. Leave a note in locker 215, if interested.

Wow....she makes it really tempting....NOT! -Gutsy

I will do this. I can be buying lots of soda with $6. Also is not so bad job. She is look like girls back home. Only with no beard.
-Mouse

Mouse and DD Grounding....The Scale of Injustice

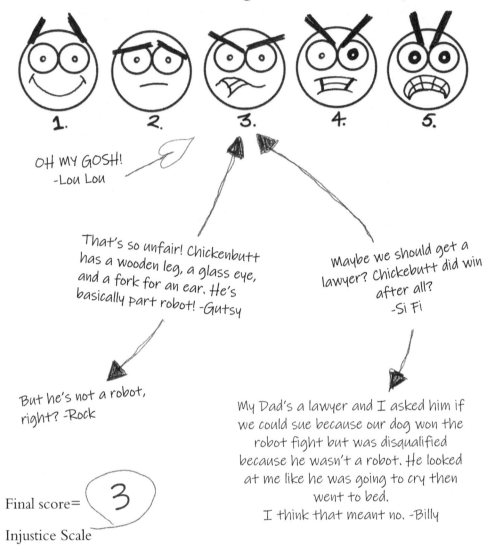

Injustice Scale

1- Dude, you were totally wrong. You deserve the grounding.

2- Alright, it was a mistake. But, dude, you were still wrong.

3- Well, that wasn't cool, was it? They didn't have to ground you for that.

4- Whoa, that's totally not right. You don't deserve to be grounded for that.

5- WHAT!? That's not fair. Stay where you are, we're coming to get you.

Free Nelson Update

by Gutsy with DD

Days Grounded: 364

Assignment: Follow the cats.

I don't know why we had to do this assignment, it's not going to help us free Nelson, or help us to stop getting grounded! We still did it…but it was stupid…..I'm just saying.

So we waited outside Nelson's house until, one of the cats left then we followed it. Here's what we found out:

Minute 1: Cat leaves Nelson's house.

Minute 2: Cat walks down the street and sits on the corner to clean itself.

Minute 20: Still cleaning itself.

Minute 25: More cleaning.

Minute 26: Cat suddenly runs across road and into the park. It leaps over bushes, springs across mud, and jumps with ease between several small trees. DD follows it and gets cuts from the bushes, dirty when he falls in the mud, and lands on his head after falling out of a tree.

Minute 35: Cat returns to the corner and sits down to clean itself again.

Minute 42: More cleaning.

Minute 43: DD starts dancing and telling me he wants to change his name to Samantha. I think he might have banged his head harder than I thought.

Minute 46: Cat walks off down street. I go to follow but DD refuses to go anywhere.

Minute 47: DD finally agrees to come with me….but only after I promise to hold his hand and read him a book before bedtime. He then starts to suck his thumb.

Minute 48: Cat walks down the main street in town.

Minute 49: Lots of people stare at me holding hands with the large boy who thinks he's a tiny baby.

Minute 52: Cat walks past girls softball practice.

Minute 53: We try to sneak past girls softball practice. One of the girls tells me I look great for someone who just had a baby.

Minute 57: Cat walks past the football team's practice.

Minute 58: We try to sneak past the football teams practice. Whole team asks where the baby's father is.

Minute 59: DD just asked me where his teddy bear is. I think he may need medical attention.

Minute 60: I realize that we may have to stop following the cat and decide to have a quick snack while I think about what to do. I take DD's candy bar and tell him that sugar is bad for him. He says, "Thank woo Daddy."

Minute 61: While I eat his candy bar I remember the time he broke a table in half with his head for a dare. Once the bleeding had stopped he was fine. I decide we should keep following the cat.

Minute 73: DD still insists on holding hands with me. Cat continues to walk past the D.I.E. Sisters, the Karate School and my Dad's office.

Minute 74: I am really starting to dislike this cat.

Minute 80: Cat goes back toward Nelson's house. I can't believe it, we could have just waited here all along.

Minute 81: At the last minute, cat turns and goes into Nelson's neighbor's house instead.

Minute 82: We read the sign on the neighbor's mailbox.

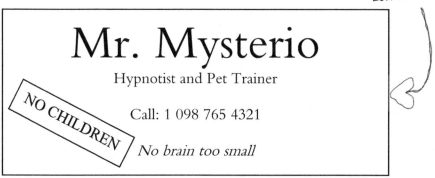

Interesting!
-Lou Lou

Minute 88: DD asks me to change his diaper for him. I decide it's time to take him to the hospital.

Well, that's what happened. I don't know what we learned....except for don't walk past people you know while holding hands with a grown boy who thinks he's a baby....it doesn't make you look cool!

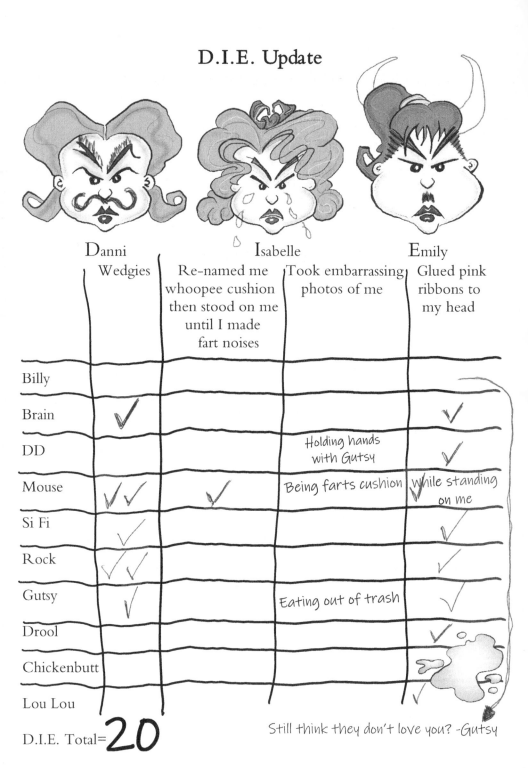

D.I.E Update....continued....

Going back into DIE's base by SiFi, with Mouse and Drool.

So, we waited outside D.I.E.'s base until we saw them leave. The diary was inside but this time we were ready! Drool had a flashlight, I had some dog treats, and Mouse had the camera. Oh, and he was wearing a wetsuit, rubber gloves and a gas mask...... I'd spent 2 hours trying to get him to explain why he was dressed like that but all he would say was, "Not again. Not after what goat did on me last time."

Drool put the key in the lock and opened the door. All of us were wishing that Chickenbutt was there with us as we waited for D.I.E.'s dog to attack us. We'd tried to get him to come but he refused to move. He just laid there, covered in silver paper, looking exhausted.

We finally got up the nerve to step inside. At first everything seemed to be just the way DD and Drool said it was; smelly, dirty,....really smelly. We waited for the attack, but nothing happened. The dog wasn't there, but there was something else. One of the couches had been pushed back opening up the wall behind it. On it had been written twelve lists that ran from floor to ceiling, each topped with some very familiar names....our names.

Nelson	Mildred	Billy	Brain
DD	Mouse	SiFi	Rock
Gutsy	Drool	Lou Lou	Chickenbutt

Beneath each name was a very long list; everything that person had been doing, where they lived, what time they went to bed, what they ate for lunch. All of it was there on the wall. I told Mouse to take a picture but before he could get the camera out we heard something. It was a key in the door. The D.I.E. Sisters were back!

All of us ran for the back door as quietly as we could....except for Mouse who's wetsuit kept making loud squeaking noises. Just as we heard D.I.E. turn the door handle we all stepped through the backdoor...............and into a bathroom?

It wasn't a backdoor after all....we were trapped! By now we could hear D.I.E. moving around their base so I turned and whispered for Drool and Mouse to be quiet. Drool looked terrified while Mouse was pointing in the toilet and whispering, "Is this what we is here for?"

Ignoring him I began looking for an escape. The only way out was a tiny window above the toilet. Drool was already halfway out before I could say anything and I pushed Mouse to follow him. Now, I don't know if you've ever tried to silently push someone in a wetsuit through a tiny window in the dark so three of your deadliest enemies don't hear you but let me tell you, it's not as easy as it sounds!

SSQQUUEEKKKKK

I jammed my shoulder against Mouse's butt and tried to push but the noise of his wetsuit against the window frame only got louder.

SSSQQQUUUEEKKK.....

Through the door I heard the voices of D.I.E. suddenly become quiet.

SSSQQQUUUEEEKKKK......

The handle to the bathroom began to slowly turn before coming to a stop. Then it was shaking violently as they realized it was locked.
SSSSSQQQQQUUUUUUEEEEEEKKKKKKK..........POP.
Mouse was finally out and instantly I scrambled out behind him. Falling out the other side I heard a loud bang, as someone kicked the door open behind me!

I'd love to say I was brave enough to look back but I just ran....and ran....and didn't stop until I was safely back at base where Drool and Mouse were waiting. The only good thing to come from the evening, was that Drool managed to get the diary after all. It seemed that while we were busy looking at the wall one of us remembered what we were there for. I couldn't be bothered to read it. Lou Lou was at our base when we got back and she was so excited that we were successful that I just gave it to her. But don't worry Billy, Im sure it says they still love you!

Oh, and one other thing. I finally find out why Mouse was wearing the wetsuit, rubber gloves and gas mask….."Oooohhh! Now is making sense!" he said when he saw the diary. "I is thinking we is here to get diarrhea!"

Chickenbutt Bath Report by Lou Lou

Chickenbutt before bath

Chickenbutt after bath.... Yeah, that's right....WOW!

Well, I hate to say that girls are better than boys but look at this!

You tried bribes, you tried lies, you even tried machines! But boys, it seems that only a girl could get this job done! You see there are a few things you all need to learn. We girls like to be treated with sensitivity. We like to be treated with caring. We like to be treated with love. And that's why Chickenbutt likes to be treated with all three of these things....because.... CHICKENBUTT IS A GIRL....!

Oh, and not only is she a girl, she is also about to have puppies!!!!

In case you're wondering who the father is, he's very much in love and has been hiding at our base all week, just to be close to Chickenbutt. This is why he wasn't there when you broke into his home to steal a diary....that's right boys, the mascot of our gang is actually a girl who will very soon be having puppies with the mascot of your worst enemies!

Oh, and here's a good thought to leave you with....if she has lots of girl puppies, there will be more girls in the gang than boys!

I thought you'd appreciate a space where you can all tell me how great I am.

I want to cry. -Gutsy

And while I have your attention, one more thing.....I thought you might like to know what D.I.E. wrote about Billy in their diary.

It's on the next page....

Thursday
 I really hate sports. Maybe I'll give a wedgie to someone on the basketball team tomorrow.

Friday
 Oh Billy. You are so perfect. How I wish that you would be my date to the dance. It's such a shame that we have to get rid of you and the rest of The Grounded Gang. Maybe I'll get a kiss....before the end!

That's all they wrote. Strangely the rest of the pages were blank. I think they may have hidden them knowing we might try to come back for the rest of the diary. But then, why did they leave this page for us to see? And what do they mean, "Get rid of us"? I think we need to worry about this.

Yeah, yeah. Look you're wasting valuable space that we could be using to make jokes about D.I.E. loving Billy! - Gutsy

Billy's a ladykiller....who's going to get killed....by a lady! -Si Fi

No, I mean it! I think this is serious! -Lou Lou

Mmmmmmm....is someone jealous perhaps? -DD

Aaaaaahhhhhhhh! -Lou Lou

What We Learned This Month by Billy

Don't ask Mouse if you can read his diary....he may show you something you really don't want to see.

Urinal cakes are not space rocks.

Killer robots should not be taken to school.

If your Dad sees you walking home with someone who thinks he is a giant baby you will have to go to therapy.

Don't presume your gang's dog is a boy.

If someone bangs their head you should really take them to hospital immediately....even if it's DD!

If you are going to break into someone's base make sure you have a lookout.

Dogs are not robots.

I am great at selling advertising.

DON'T TRUST OUR ENEMIES....EVER!

Stuff We Didn't Get Grounded For This Month

I spilled my Dad's shampoo. -Drool

That's not so bad! -Brain

I didn't want to get in trouble so I filled it back up with another bottle I found in the bathroom. -Drool

So, that's still not so bad. It's actually quite considerate. -Brain

I filled it up with hair remover cream by accident. -Drool

Oooooooohhhhhhhh!!!! - Brain

Dad doesn't need shampoo anymore. Just some polish to make his head all shiny! -Billy

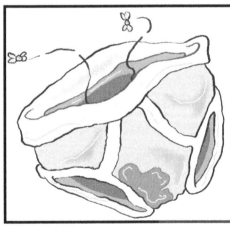

Need Underpants? Buy Mine!

Only worn ~~for a week~~ once.
Slight smell but you soon get used to it.
Asking 50 cents. Or will swap for clean underpants.
Contact locker 916 for details.

Locker 916? Isn't that yours Rock? - Gutsy

Maybe....why, are you interested in buying them? I can arrange for you to try them on if you're interested. -Rock

Final Thoughts by Billy

So, not exactly the best month. Half the gang's grounded, our manly mascot is actually a pretty girl mascot, and I am suddenly irresistible to one of the D.I.E. Sisters! Just when I thought things were getting better, life kicks us down again! You know all that noise that the workmen keep making in our neighborhood? Well, yesterday they moved their little orange tent outside my house. So, I peeked in to see what was so important that they needed to keep banging away at all hours and you know what happened? I was attacked by a cat! I'd hardly put my hand on the tent door when this crazy ball of fur jumps on my head and starts scratching me!

Interesting! - Lou Lou

Anyway, I managed to escape while I still had some hair left but I'd recommend no-one go near that tent, even if the banging noise is driving you crazy!

Oh, one last thing, Lou Lou has requested that I give you all a quick reminder to keep the base tidy. It seems someone left blood stains all over the couch and a pile of candy wrappers under one of the cushions. Also, if anyone has a first aid kit at home could they bring it to the base? I cut my finger on a bag of chocolate gumballs last week and we had no band aids so in the end I just had to wipe it on the....oh....gotta go. - Billy

No, it's not interesting, it was very painful.....and will you stop saying that everything is interesting!? —Billy

Assignments for Next Month by Billy

<u>D.I.E. Update</u>- As your brave, fearless leader, I have decided to take this assignment. I plan on using my good looks and charm to find out exactly what they meant when they said they planned on getting rid of us. No-one talks about my gang like that!

Do you think he wants to know which D.I.E. sister likes him? - Gutsy

<u>Free Nelson Update</u>- Brain. I need for you to work out a way to get us into the school office. If we can get a good look at Nelson's permanent record, then maybe we can work out why he's grounded. If whatever he did was bad enough to get him grounded this long, then it should be in his file....I know, clever right!? Alright, so maybe Lou Lou came up with the idea, but I still had to approve it.

Sounds like it. But at least he hasn't let it go to his head! - Lou Lou

<u>Chickenbutt Bath/Baby Update</u> – Lou Lou. You're a girl, Chickenbutt's a girl. We're boys, what do we know about babies!? So, can you take care of the whole birth thing? Please NO PICTURES! It sounds totally gross!

<u>Drinks and Snacks/Fundraising-</u> Everyone meet me at lunchtime, Monday.

<u>Protect the Base-</u> Well, we have no security anymore. Let's hope someone doesn't break in and mess the place up, (please).

GROUNDED GANG OUT!!!!

I have an Idea! -Billy

Grounded Gang Out!

Gutsy

Rock   DD

Billy   Lou Lou

Drool
(Chickenbutt)

Mouse   Si Fi

February

And...I sold another one! -Billy

February Meeting by Billy

I'm no genius but think I would have noticed if someone was living under me! - Rock

Letter from The President,

Okay guys, I have two words for you....lunchbox basketball! Just in case you've been living under a rock, let me explain. You know how every lunchtime kids play lunchbox basketball? Well, I've been watching them, and think I might have a way for us to make some money. Okay, let me explain some more. In lunchbox basketball two kids play basketball against each other, but instead of using a ball they use things from their lunchboxes.

Each kid gets three shots and the winner gets the other kid's lunchbox for a week. The loser? Well, that part's not so good! The loser has to eat all the things that were used as balls. So, if it's a turkey sandwich that's been mushed against the backboard, they have to eat it. If it's a bag of chips that exploded when it hit the floor, they have to eat it. Trust me, you don't want to lose this game.

Anyway, I was hanging out at the base last week and Lou Lou was there eating peanuts. So, I was watching and I saw that she threw the shells into the trash. But get this, the trash was all the way across the room and she never missed, not even once. I'm telling you, she's like some sort of wizard!

So, here's what I thought. We give Lou Lou all our lunchboxes and she uses them to beat all the kids at school and win us a bunch of food for the week. We then sell that food back to the kids who lost and we'll have ourselves a fortune! Now I know what you're thinking, "There's no way she'll do it!" But get this, I asked her already and she agreed! I'm telling you, having Lou Lou in the gang might actually pay off after all!

Anyway, meet me tomorrow morning, before school, and give me your lunchboxes. I'll put a report of how it goes on the end of this month's meeting. Trust me guys. We're going to be rich!

You're an idiot! - Lou Lou

Did you ever think that if you put as much effort into finding out why you keep getting grounded as you do into trying to get money for soda and candy your life might be a lot easier! -Lou Lou

Thinking bad. Soda good. Candy better! -DD

Grounded Gang Central

Stuff for February

Roll Call

Secret Smell of the Month

Password for the Month

New Clubhouse Rules

Grounded.......or Why I'm Not There

Scale of Injustice

Free Nelson Update

D.I.E. Update

Chickenbutt Baby Report

Stuff We Didn't Get Grounded For This Month

What We Learned This Month

Final Thoughts

Assignments for Next Month

Rollcall

	HERE	GROUNDED
Nelson		✓
Billy	✓	
Brain		✓
Double Dare	✓	
Mouse	✓	
Si Fi	✓	
Rock		✓
Gutsy	✓	
Lou Lou	✓	
Drool	✓	
Chickenbutt	(Chickenbutt)	

Secret Smell of the Month....by Mouse

So, I is thinking I is doing somethings nice by bringing in a secrets smells that we can all eats too! Is called Blavornaschnoogle and it is being the food of my country. Is made of fish eyesballs, seaweed, onions, garlic, hot sauce, pigs foot, and ketchup! Is tasting so goods and is smellings even betters. It is remindings me of home and me is no embarressed to says that's when I smells it a little bit of water comes in my eyes. So enjoys! Is my gifts to you alls to show hows much I likes beings in your gangs. Of course I is liking its much mores when we is no grounded. Blavornaschnoogle!

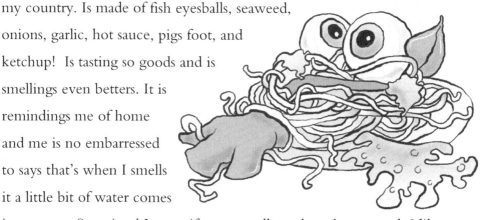

It smells like he cooked it in a gym sock! -Billy

I think he invented a food that can kill you without you having to eat it. -Brain

Must get fresh air please help

Password for the Month

This months password will be:

Gil. T

which we are not! Billy

New Clubhouse Rules

	YES	NO
Anyone eating peanut butter with their hands is not allowed to be in charge of the remote. -Billy	✓	✓
Si Fi's telescope is to be used for looking for aliens only. It is definitely not for sword fights, itches you can't reach, or unblocking the toilet! -Si Fi	✓	✓✓✓✓
There's something dead behind the TV and it has a bunch of wires attached to it! Somebody, please remove it. It smells terrible! -Lou Lou	✓	✓
If I have an experiment in progress, that is wired up to the TV, please do not touch it! I'm bringing something back to life. -Brain	✓	✓
Oh, and don't use channel 666 on the TV........at least not yet.... -Brain	✓✓✓	✓✓
If anyone found peanut butter on the remote control let me know. I would like it back. -Gutsy	✓	
Any dead pets buried behind the base must not be used for experiments. Mr. Snuffles, why did you have to leave so soon......why?! -Drool		✓
Maybe, it's because you forgot to feed him for a month! -Billy	✓	
Oh, yeah, never mind....I have a goldfish now. -Drool	✓	
This is amazing country. Even your remotes taste like peanuts butters. I likes very much. -Mouse.		✓

Grounded....Or Why I'm Not There by Brain with Rock

Name: Brain and Rock
Status: Grounded
Reason: I put my nose in your lunch!

So, our assignment was to get Nelson's file from the school to see why he'd been grounded. And, once again my plan was totally genius! I decided to disguise someone as a health inspector visiting the school kitchen. All the files are kept in a storage area behind the kitchen so while everyone was busy with the Health Inspector I was going to slip into the storage area, unseen, and find Nelsons file. It was foolproof....but, unfortunately not Rockproof! Okay, I know that I said I would never work with Rock on anymore assignments. And I know that, technically, this time it's my fault because I asked him to help. But, I needed someone big and tall to pretend to be the health inspector and Rock is bigger and taller than anyone else in our gang. What was I going to do? Take Drool and pretend the health inspector was four feet tall with three teeth and a girl's voice? Besides, the plan was so simple that even Rock couldn't mess it up. At least that's what I thought!

Hey....I mean HEY! – Drool

The first thing we needed was a disguise. Well, let's just say that in this department I outdid myself,....again!

In the past few month I've created my own polymere rubber solution. It looks just like the modeling clay we used to play with in art class, only

100 times better! All you have to do is mold it into a mask, wait ten minutes, and the mask looks like it has perfect human skin. I'm telling you, it's amazing and, it makes a brilliant disguise! Using my polymere rubber solution, I'd made a mask for Rock that was undetectable. After he put it on not even his own Mom could have recognize him! I'd even built a little receiver into the ear so I could hear everything he said or heard. Im telling you, I should have been a spy!

Don't call it poly want a cracker solution. He doesn't find it funny. -Rock

BEFORE

AFTER

The plan was all set for Friday. So, at lunchtime Rock, or Mr. Burger as he was now called, walked up to Gas and the lunch ladies and told them he was he was there to inspect the kitchen. An instant look of fear spread on their faces and while they were distracted, I slipped under one of the empty food carts and waited. I didn't have to wait long before

Theres only three things that scare lunch ladies.
1. Eating their own cooking
2. Mirrors
3. Health Inspectors

– Billy

someone pushed me into the kitchen and to the back of the room....right where I wanted to be!

In my ear I heard Gas talking to Rock and, while he kept her busy, I slipped out from under the cart and into the storage area, where I quickly began searching for Nelson's file.

My plan was going perfectly....but, then Rock started to talk. You see Rock had been under strict instructions to just be nice. He didn't need to tell Gas her food was disgusting, that's just rude....and obvious. All he had to do was go in there, distract her with compliments about what a great job she was doing, and give me enough time to get in and out with the file. Instead, I hear this;   *I got hungry!- Rock*

"I'd like to see what you're cooking today. It smells.....strange."

Instantly, my heart froze. Okay, maybe I should of mentioned this earlier. You see, my perfect invention isn't quite so perfect after all. The polymere solution is great....but not if you put it near heat. And kitchens can be a little hot. That's why Rock had been told to stay away from the stove....   *Poly want a cracker! Sorry I couldn't help myself.- Rock*

"Is this beef stew on the stove?" said Rock, "let me smell it!"

I knew this was going to be bad. Quickly I flicked through the files, desperately thinking of ways to warn Rock that he was about to do something really stupid. But, at that moment, he was already leaning over a huge, steaming bowl of bubbling stew.

"Tell me what's in this," said Rock. The silence, that followed, let me know something bad had happened and so I quickly grabbed a handful of files before running for the door. The scream that greeted me, when I got there told me that I was too late!

"AAAaaaaaaaaaahhhhhhhhhhhhh!!!!!!!!!!!!!!!!!!!!"

I peeked out to see Rock looking up from the steaming stew....at a terrified group of lunch ladies. Only he didn't look Rock.... and he didn't look like Mr. Burger. In fact, he didn't look like anything I'd ever seen before. The mask I'd made for him wasn't there. Instead, his face looked like it's been made out of modeling clay....by a kindergartener....in the dark....using only their feet.

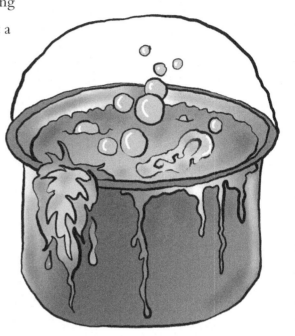

Large blobs were dripping from his nose as his ear slowly peeled itself off, before landing with a 'plop' in the stew. More screams followed as the lunch ladies began shouting, "I knew that was beef was old," and "we've killed another one!" That was when I decided it was time for a new plan called 'Get Out Of Here Now!' So, I took off running across the kitchen. Only Rock caught sight of me and turned to see what I was doing.

I thought it tasted better than usual that day! -Gutsy

But this made what was left of his mask fly across the room. Where it hit me....right in the face.

So now the lunch ladies were looking at two kids with melting faces. And one of them screamed, "Quick! Before the police get here, hide the pudding!"

Out of the corner of my eye I saw Gas slipping into the back storage room as if she knew I'd been in there. Then I heard the kitchen door open. Immediately the screaming stopped and I peeled a piece of Mr. Burgers face off my glasses….only to see The Law, scowling at me and Rock. That was it. Before I knew it we were in The Hammer's office listening to him tell our parents all about how we'd impersonated health inspectors and tried to poison the school food. I joked that this was technically impossible as most of the school food was already poison but, I don't think he thought it was very funny. I know this because he screamed, "THAT'S NOT FUNNY!"

Interesting. – Lou Lou

So, now we're grounded and I'm stuck in my bedroom listening to all the workmen outside….again. And to make it worse the files I got were useless. Nelson's was blank, except for some silly notes and I didn't even look at the other ones. I'll put them in the book but don't hold your breath. They won't help us at all.

Oh, just in case I ever forget again…….I DO NOT WANT TO BE PAIRED UP WITH ROCK EVER AGAIN!

EVER! -Brain   EVER! -Brain   EVER! -Brain

Conclusion: Brain and Rock grounded for three weeks each.

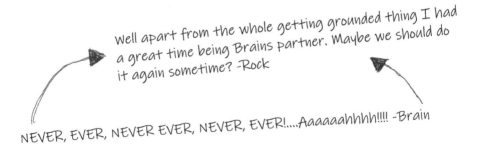

Well apart from the whole getting grounded thing I had a great time being Brains partner. Maybe we should do it again sometime? -Rock

NEVER, EVER, NEVER EVER, NEVER, EVER!....Aaaaaahhhh!!!! -Brain

Grounded Evidence #1:

TOP SECRET

The file of Nelson Delly has been moved to the special projects file:

Codename:
OPERATION GOLDENMIND

Delly, Nelson

What the heck! Where's his file? -Billy

I think someone doesn't want us to know why Nelson's grounded....I wonder why? -Lou Lou

Grounded Evidence #2:

School Kitchen....TOP SECRET!

Dear Principal Mallet,

Here is the list of ingredients we have been using to feed the students. With all the money we're saving we should be able to have a great staff party at the end of the year! -Mildred Mulberry

MENU	REAL MENU
Fish Sticks……...	Bits of old fish, and sticks.
Peas……………	Bits from bottom of hamster cage.
Cheese Pizza…..	Gym socks, ketchup and hairnets.
Chili……………	Janitor's mop bucket left overs.
Mac & Cheese....	Cockroaches in old cheese.
Baked Ziti……..	Cockroaches in ketchup.
Popcorn Chicken..	Rats feet.
Chicken Fingers…	Rats tails.
Chicken Nuggets...	All the other rat bits.
Chicken Meatballs...	CENSORED

NOTE: Don't worry. We serve the real food at the teachers table. And to the D.I.E. Sisters....of course!

Kitchen - TOP SECRET

Trust me. Do not look under there! -Billy

I looked and I have to say. I'd still eat it. - Gutsy

Dude, you eat toenails....even if they aren't yours! -Billy

Grounded Evidence #3:

Brain and Rocks Grounding....The Scale of Injustice

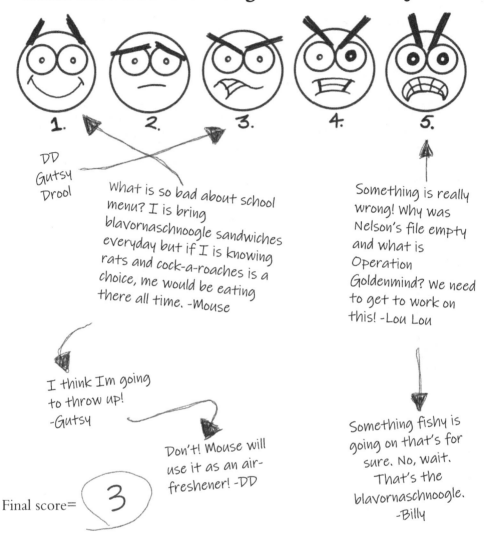

Injustice Scale

1- Dude, you were totally wrong. You deserve the grounding.

2- Alright, it was a mistake. But, dude, you were still wrong.

3- Well, that wasn't cool, was it? They didn't have to ground you for that.

4- Whoa, that's totally not right. You don't deserve to be grounded for that.

5- WHAT!? That's not fair. Stay where you are, we're coming to get you.

Free Nelson Update

by Billy....'cause Brain isn't here!

Days Grounded: 392

Mission: Brain to break into the school and get Nelson's file to discover why he has been grounded....let's not re-live it again. Let's just say, it didn't go well....so, instead, here's a commercial for Lester's Lunch in a tube. It's delicious, nutritious, and he paid me an extra 50 cents to say that.

D.I.E. Update

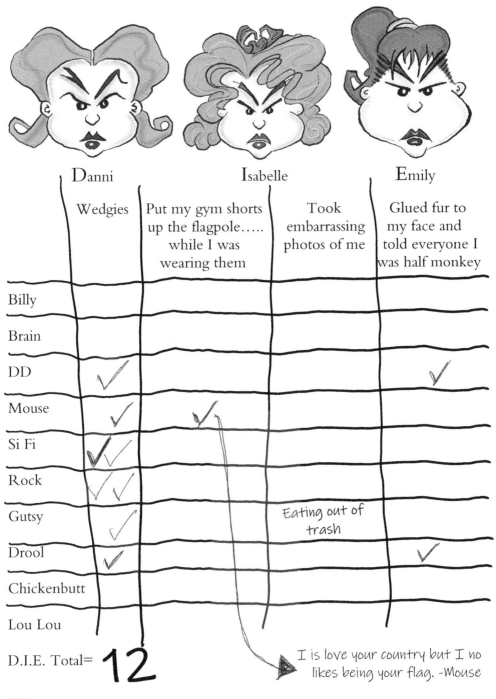

	Danni	Isabelle	Emily
	Wedgies	Put my gym shorts up the flagpole….. while I was wearing them	Took embarrassing photos of me	Glued fur to my face and told everyone I was half monkey
Billy				
Brain				
DD	✓			✓
Mouse	✓	✓		
Si Fi	✓			
Rock	✓			
Gutsy	✓		Eating out of trash	
Drool	✓			✓
Chickenbutt				
Lou Lou				

D.I.E. Total= **12**

I is love your country but I no likes being your flag. -Mouse

D.I.E. Update....continued....by Billy

What can I say? We needed information, and if you need information from the D.I.E. Sisters, you have to find their weakness. And, I happen to be their weakness! You've read their diary, they love me! I'm like kryptonite to them, they just go weak when they're around me!

So, I was thinking about the best way to get the information I wanted. Then I thought, 'hey, just tell them to leave us alone, let your good looks do all the work for you!' So, that's what I did. I went to talk to them where they like to hang out after school....behind the dumpster, torturing kids.

"Hi beautiful ladies," I said. You could tell they were in awe of me because Emily stopped giving a wet willy to the third grader she had in a head lock and Danni and Isabelle both dropped the fourth grader with the fresh wedgie. Then, they all looked at me in a way that can only be described by one word................H O T. Oh yes, they are in love with me, no doubt about it.

"Listen ladies," it's time to end this war between us," I said, "how about you keep away from my gang and I'll let you keep using me as eye candy?" Well, you could tell they were impressed. They couldn't even speak.

"I'll consider this a done deal," I said. Then, I winked and smiled,...just a little bit,...I didn't want to drive them too crazy! Then, I walked away real slow, so they had something good to look at.

Let's just say, I think they'll be giving us a lot less trouble in the future!

D.I.E. Update....continued....continued....by Billy

Now, here is a blank page for you all to use, to thank me, and tell me just how great I am....................

Extra bit by Drool.............
Yeah, instead, why don't I use this space to say what really happened? You see, I had to walk home with Billy so I saw it all.....unfortunately! So, the bit about Billy talking to the D.I.E. Sisters is true. But, not the bit about them being in love with him. I think he only survived because they were in shock that he even talked to them in the first place! Plus, there's an extra bit that Billy forgot to mention. When he was walking away, real slow, he tripped over his shoelaces and fell head first into one of the dumpsters. And not just any dumpster, the one that The Mop uses for trash from Needles office. I don't think the D.I.E. Sisters were ever in love with him, and especially not now they've seen him covered in used band-aids and old tissues. There is good news though...I took a picture!

Drool, you are so dead! -Billy

D.I.E. Update....continued....continued.... by Lou Lou

Errrrr........Billy, I hate to do this but after you said you were going to deal with D.I.E. on your own, I thought it would be a good idea to check their diary again.

It seems that there was an extra page that I missed.....sorry!

> MONDAY
>
> We've decided we don't like Billy anymore. We saw him scratch his butt then eat one of his boogers yesterday....totally gross! If the boss didn't want us to stay away from him, we'd give him the wedgie to end all wedgies. But, we'll just have to save it until the boss says it's time to get rid of him!

Oh yeah! You're like kryptonite....if kryptonite ate it's own poopy boogers!
-DD

On the plus side we now know that there's a boss who controls them. Now we just need to work out who it is!
-Lou Lou

Chickenbutt Bath Baby Report by Lou Lou

So, great news! I am very happy to report that Ms. Chickenbutt gave birth to eight wonderful puppies last week! Mommy, Daddy, and puppies are all doing well. I know you said no photos but I couldn't help myself.

Aren't they just the cutest thing ever!
-Lou Lou

Are those dogs or Halloween masks?
-DD

The best news is that I think I've found good homes for them all! My Uncle has a farm and he says he'll adopt them! In the meantime, they need a place to stay so, each of us will need to take one home until he can fetch them. Don't worry....they are no trouble at all. Don't get too attached though. They are awfully cute!

What We Learnt This Month.

Don't be goings on dates with girls for soda moneys. I is doing only what she said and now she is follows me everywhere! She is even tryings to bribes me with free sodas so I will go out with her agains! She is likes crazy goat! -Mouse

That's terrible! What are you going to do? -DD

We is going to movies tonight. -Mouse

WHAT?!?!?!? -DD

She is paying for super large soda....oh, and you is being chickenbutts! -Mouse

I learned not to eat gummy bears from a jar. Especially if you later find out that they are you Mom's fiber supplements. -Gutsy

Fiber....that makes you go....you know? -Brain

Oh, I know! -Gutsy

The one-a-day fiber gummies? How many did you eat? - Brain

144 -Gutsy

Oh, so you've been..... -Brain

That's all I've been doing! I think I'd rather have been attacked by a real bear! -Gutsy

Stuff We Didn't Get Grounded For....

I borrowed fake dog poop from our base and put it on The Mallets front doorstep! -Si Fi

I borrowed fake dog poop from our base and put it outside The Mops cleaning closet! -Rock

I borrowed fake dog poop from our base and put it on The Laws desk! -Gutsy

Wait....we don't have any fake dog poop at our base, do we? -Billy

???? -Si Fi

Sorry guys, I brought the puppies by to visit the base last week. They must have had some accidents....I think that might have been real dog poop! -Lou Lou

On man! I touched poop! -Si Fi

Think yourself lucky. I carried mine to school in my pocket! -Gutsy

Oh no!...I hid mine in my lunchbox.... -Rock

Final Thoughts by Billy

Well things, still, just aren't going our way, are they? We keep trying to get to the bottom of everything but it never works. It's as if something big is going on right under our noses....but someone doesn't want us to see....so, they keep getting us in trouble! Like some sort of conspiracy.

Well, that's what Lou Lou says she thinks it is. I don't know where she gets the idea that there are pirates involved. I haven't seen any pirates around our neighborhood. But, there's no point in upsetting her by telling her she's wrong, not with the big lunchbox basketball game coming up.

I can read you know?! -Lou Lou

We are going to win big....I just know it! And when we do, we'll have money again; money we can use to further our investigation into why all the teachers and D.I.E. hate us so much. Just kidding. That's just what Lou Lou wants to do with it. I say we spend it on soda and video games. The big lunchbox basketball game is tomorrow. Don't forget to give me your lunchboxes in the morning. I'll let you know how it goes.

Again, I can read! -Lou Lou

-Billy

Assignments for Next Month by Billy

<u>D.I.E. Update</u>- Drool, as you are so good at taking photos of people without them knowing, why don't you follow the D.I.E. Sisters and get some pictures we can blackmail them with? Lets hope they don't get their hands on you....

<u>Free Nelson Update</u>- Everyone else. May is only two months away and if we don't solve this soon, Nelson might end up grounded for another whole summer! That's why you are all doing 'Free Nelson' this month. Your job is to get a hold of one of the collars from the crazy cats. I know it sounds dangerous but, trust me, it's important....alright, I don't know why it's important either, but Lou Lou says it is and she won't play lunchbox basketball unless we do it so, good luck!

<u>Chickenbutt Bath Birth Babies Update</u> – Be here tomorrow when Lou Lou will bring in the puppies. We all have to look after one each until her Uncles in town. It should be fun. At least that's what she said it would be.

<u>Drinks and Snacks/Fundraising</u> -No worries! Lunchbox basketball = money!

<u>Protect the Base-</u> The place will be full of weird looking puppies soon. I don't think security will be a problem.

Grounded Gang Out!

Billy

Si Fi

Gutsy

Drool

DD

Lou Lou

Mouse

(Chickenbutt)

An extra bit....Lunchbox Basketball Update by Billy

I knew it! I said it would work. Didn't I say it would work? I'm a genius! Okay, Lou Lou was kinda great too. You should have seen her, she never missed a shot! Banana shots, chip shots, sandwich shots, juice box shots, cookie shots, apple shots, liver paste shots, even a watermelon shot! You should have seen the other kids faces. One by one they kept coming, all of them convinced they could beat a girl. But one by one she beat them, leaving them to eat what was left of their missed shots. And now, for the rest of the week, they all have to give me their lunchboxes everyday ....which I will then sell back to them at a very nice profit! By the weekend we'll have enough money for us to get a new video game AND two crates of soda AND have so much left over that we can open an account for us at the bank, at the end of our street! But that's not even the best bit. You see, as Lou Lou was beating every kid in school, I thought of a genius plan. And that's when I challenged the D.I.E. Sisters to a game....and they agreed! Admittedly, the stakes are a little bit bigger than I would have liked but it was Lou Lou's idea, and hey, she can't lose! She's playing them on Monday. If we win they have to leave us alone, forever. And if they win we have to swap bases with them. But don't worry......she can't lose. And by this time next week, the D.I.E. Sisters will be just a memory!

> Who eats liver paste? -DD

> I do's. You should trys. Is good for you's. Is tasting like chicken. Especially the chicken ones. -Mouse

> I'll try it! -Gutsy

He is sellings another one? Please tells me I don't have to dates this one two?........Is she having any soda? -Mouse

March

For Sale. My Big Sister.

She's got too much homework.

She broke up with her boyfriend.

She has a new zit.

She thinks she's fat.

She keeps crying for no reason.

She's my big sister and she's all yours....please take her away.......
for free.....Please.....I cant take her anymore. She's killing me......HELP!
Locker 96

March Meeting by Billy

NO!

Lunchbox Basketball Update by Billy

What happened? I still don't get it! She was supposed to be impossible to beat! But, out walked the D.I.E. Sisters and, suddenly, she can't hit a shot to save her life! Everything missed! Cheese cubes, carrots, brownies, crackers, strawberries. She couldn't even score with an apple! Even worse, I'd agreed to eat all her missed shots for her. Now, I don't know which one of you had a liver and onion sandwich but, I can only say that it tastes even more disgusting after its been mashed against a basketball net before landing in a dirty puddle! Oh, and it also turns out that Im allergic to liver. So, I woke up next morning to find that my head was twice its normal size. So, thanks to whomever brought that! And now we've had to switch bases! Now I know you're all mad at me but, I didn't want to make that bet! It was Lou Lou! And guess who's suddenly been grounded and can't be here? Lou Lou! So, really, you should be mad at her! Well, I'll say sorry for her. There, I'm glad that's behind us and we've forgiven each other.

Now, we can get on with moving into our new base. I know it's not all lovely and nice like our old one but, I'm sure we can make it just as nice...maybe even better! We just need to come up with some ideas on how to make it nicer.

Its my new favorite! You have to try it. I love liver! -Gutsy

It was pretty big to begin with! -Drool

Did you get a special stamp made? -Billy

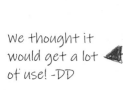

We thought it would get a lot of use! -DD

Thoughts on our Base....continued by Billy

Okay, I see you need some time....

Let's just go to the next page shall we?

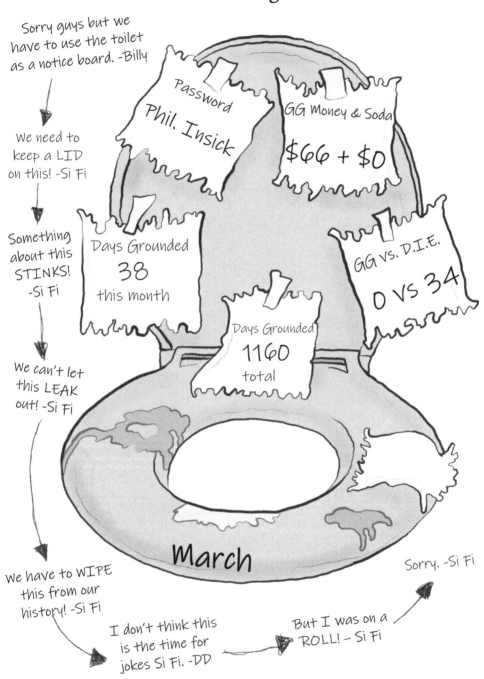

Stuff for March by Billy

Roll Call

Secret Smell of the Month

Password for the Month

New Clubhouse Rules

Grounded…….or Why I'm Not There

Scale of Injustice

Free Nelson Update

D.I.E. Update

Chickenbutt Bath/Puppies Report

Stuff We Didn't Get Grounded For This Month

What We Learned This Month

Final Thoughts

Assignments for Next Month

Has anyone else noticed how quiet it's been around here lately?
– Drool

That's because Lou Lou's grounded so there's been no girls here. - DD

Yeah. No girl's rules! - Gutsy

Of course it could be because we no longer have a TV.- Brain

T.V….why did you have to go….why? Oh, yeah. It's because of Billy. -Drool

BILLY IS OFFICIALLY NOT FORGIVEN - GG

Rollcall

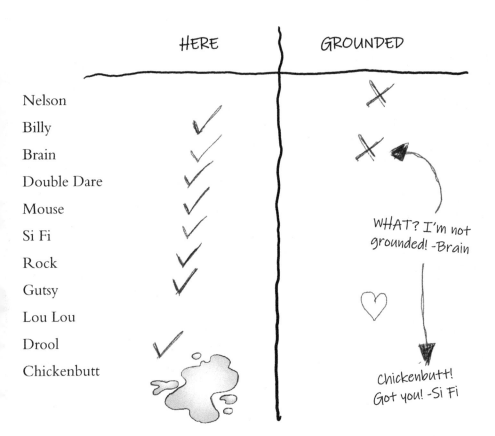

Secret Smell of the Month....by Brain

How to make this base smell better? I think that might just be impossible. I thought girls were supposed to smell like flowers and perfume. This place smells like Mr. and Mrs. Fart had a baby called Fart and the whole Fart Family came over and farted to celebrate. Science isn't advanced enough yet to remove the smell of the D.I.E. Sisters. The only thing I can do is install my latest invention; The Stink-o-Sensor! It detects three levels of smell:

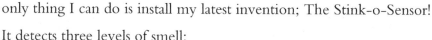

Level 1: Bad (armpits, feet, burps).
Level 2: Really Bad (farts, butt sweat, yesterday's underwear).
Level 3: Really Really Bad. (I'm going to die. Call an ambulance).
If the smell in the base ever reaches level 3, an alarm will sound. I suggest you run.

What's that beeping...? Must get to fresh air. Room getting dark. Oh, No! Not again

Password for the Month

This month's password will be:

Phil. Insick.

That would be because of the smell. -Si Fi

Clubhouse Rules

	YES	NO
Let's try to make the best of our new base. -Billy	✓	✓✓✓✓
Don't sit on the couch. You'll get a rash. -DD	✓✓✓	
Don't stand up for too long. The mold on the ceiling makes your head itchy. -Drool	✓✓✓	
Don't bring any food to the base. The rats will attack you. -Gutsy	✓✓✓	
Don't be make any loud noises. Something unders the couch growls when you do. -Mouse	✓✓✓	
Try not to breathe in here for too long. The smell seems to cause temporary blindness. -Brain	✓✓✓	
You're not ready to make the best of our new base yet, are you? -Billy		✓✓✓✓
It'll be a while before you forgive me, for this won't it? -Billy		✓✓✓✓✓

BILLY IS OFFICIALLY NOT FORGIVEN - GG

See? Told you it was a good investment! -DD

Grounded.... or Why I'm Not There by Lou Lou

Name: Lou Lou
Status: Grounded
Reason: The D.I.E. Sisters are a recipe for disaster!

Okay, so not only am I grounded but, I also have to help my Mom in the kitchen as a punishment.

And before any of you say it, just because I'm a girl it doesn't mean I like cooking, so yes, it is a punishment! Besides, it's not even cooking. I just have to sit there and write out all of her favorite recipes for her.

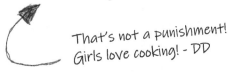

That's not a punishment! Girls love cooking! - DD

I left a big space there to test you. If any of you wrote anything in there that's offensive to women then, you are in big trouble!

Right so here's why I was grounded....

Never write in pen. Always use pencil.
Stupid! Stupid! Stupid! - DD

Next page.

Lou Lou's Recipe for Getting Grounded by Lou Lou

Ingredients

3 D.I.E. Sisters.   3 large tubes of crazy glue   1 Me -Lou Lou

1 Pledge of Allegiance   1 The Law with extra big butt

Directions:

1. Have the D.I.E. Sisters buy three tubes of crazy glue.
2. Allow them to sit overnight thinking about what to do with glue.
3. Get them to school early so they can cover my chair with glue.
4. Leave for 5 minutes so it's nice and extra sticky.
5. Slowly wait as they watch me sit down for the start of class.
6. Leave for 5 minutes to allow glue to really dry.
7. Wait for The Hammer to announce over the intercom that it's time for the Pledge of Allegiance.
8. Carefully watch as I stand up and leave my pants behind!
9. Be sure I'm wearing embarrassing underwear; unicorns & monkeys.
10. Add The Law looking up to see me doing the Pledge of Allegiance while wearing no pants.
11. Quickly proceed to the Principal's office where I am served a very hot reception!

Me has those too! But I prefer mermaids and hearts. They is my favorite. -Mouse

Lou Lou's Grounding.... The Scale of Injustice

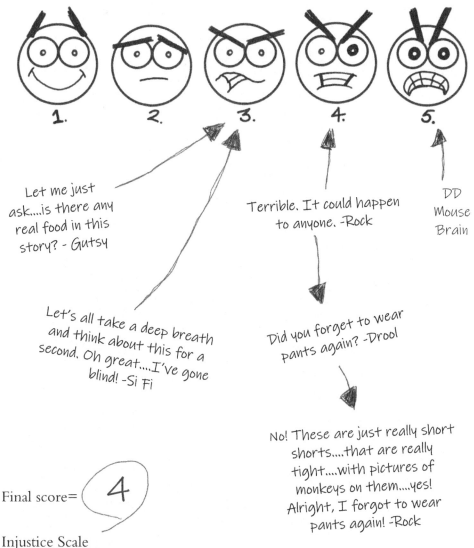

Let me just ask....is there any real food in this story? - Gutsy

Terrible. It could happen to anyone. -Rock

DD Mouse Brain

Let's all take a deep breath and think about this for a second. Oh great....I've gone blind! -Si Fi

Did you forget to wear pants again? -Drool

No! These are just really short shorts....that are really tight....with pictures of monkeys on them....yes! Alright, I forgot to wear pants again! -Rock

Final score = 4

Injustice Scale

1- Dude, you were totally wrong. You deserve the grounding.

2- Alright, it was a mistake. But dude, you were still wrong.

3- Well, that wasn't cool, was it? They didn't have to ground you for that.

4- Whoa, that's totally not right. You don't deserve to be grounded for that.

5- WHAT!? That's not fair. Stay where you are, we're coming to get you.

Free Nelson Update

by Billy, Brain, Si Fi, Mouse, Gutsy, DD

Days Grounded: 423

Assignment: Try to get one of the neighborhood cat's collars. Our results!

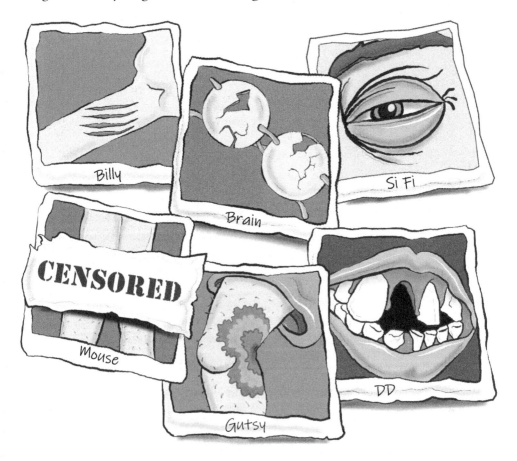

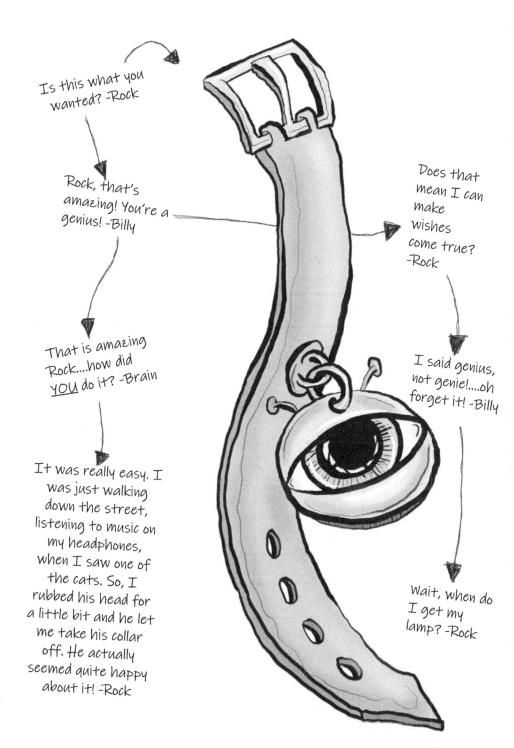

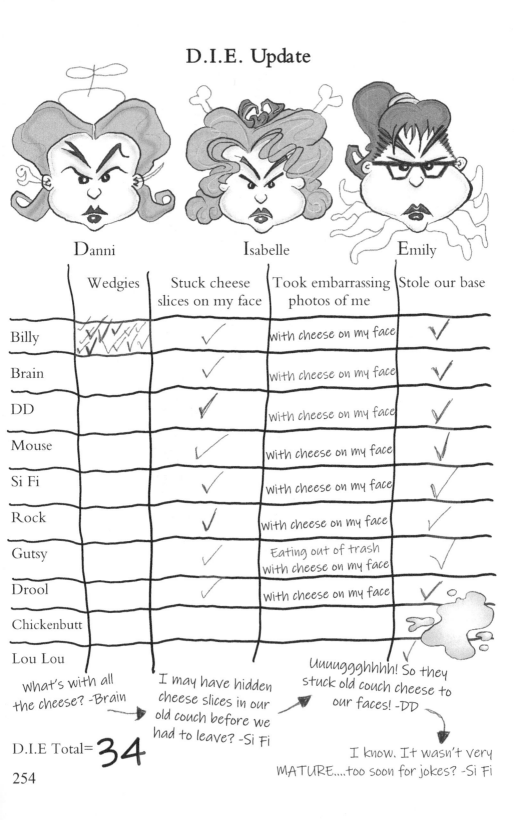

D.I.E. Update....continued....by Drool

Assignment: To get photos of the D.I.E. Sisters to blackmail them with.

I did it! I got a photo we can use to get them.....look! -Drool

What? Where is it? I thought you said you got a photo. -Billy

I did! I'm telling you there's a photo! I put it in the book myself! -Drool

Sure you did....is this like your 'friend', Tommy Tum Tum? Is this photo imaginary...just like him? -Billy

Don't you dare bring Tommy Tum Tum into this! -Drool

Like I'm supposed to forget about your imaginary friend Tommy Tum Tum! What was he again? Oh yeah, that's right, wasn't he a flying gorilla? -Drool

He didn't fly....he had a jetpack.... -Drool

Can I meet him? -Rock

Me too! Is long time since I see flying gorilla. Is makings me homesick! -Mouse

What country do you come from?! -Brain

Chickenbutt Bath Baby Puppies Report by Lou Lou

Dear Gang,
Okay boys, well obviously I'm grounded!....So I've made arrangements for my friend Susan to drop off the puppies. Pick one each to take home until I can come get them. I'd love to keep them all with me but, there's a horrid orange construction tent outside my house and the noise is upsetting the puppies. You should only need to keep them for a few days....hopefully. There's a list of their names and how to take care of them on the next page. Be nice to them, boys. They're just babies after all!

Oh, and sorry about losing lunchbox basketball....and the whole 'having to switch bases' thing. I guess it just wasn't my day! Try not to worry too much. I have an idea that things will be changing for the better very soon. Oh, and while you're in D.I.E.'s base you should have a look around. Maybe you'll find something....useful!

-Lou Lou

Yeah, what's your idea of things getting better? Will we all have to start going to school naked? -Gutsy

I told you's I is homesick. Why you has to keep reminding me of all things I miss? -Mouse.

Forget country....what planet do you come from?! -Brain

Interesting? -Si Fi

BILLY IS OFFICIALLY NOT FORGIVEN - GG

BILLY IS OFFICIALLY NOT FORGIVEN - GG

BILLY IS OFFICIALLY NOT FORGIVEN - GG

How To Take Care Of The Puppies by Lou Lou

- Feed them twice a day.

   What do puppies eat anyway? I'm not sharing my food! -Gutsy

- Make sure they have clean water.

  Why? Do they like to go swimming? -Rock

- Take them outside regularly so they can use the bathroom.

   Good! I no wants to share my trash can with pupeyes. -Mouse

- If they have a 'bathroom accident' be nice to them.

   What's a bathroom accident?....Hey, does that mean me picking up.....that's disgusting! -Drool

- Above all give them lots and lots of love!

  Yeah, right! -DD

Their names are-

Mr. Snuffles.	Wrinkly Bear	Snuggly
Cutiepie	Hiccup	Puddles
Scooter	Splat	

 I'm not walking round with any dog with one of these names! I've got a reputation to protect! We'll just have to rename them..... -Billy

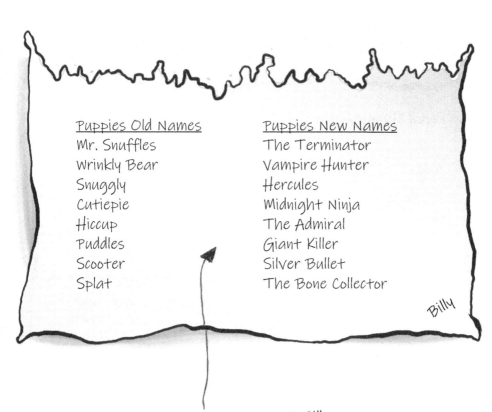

Puppies Old Names	Puppies New Names
Mr. Snuffles	The Terminator
Wrinkly Bear	Vampire Hunter
Snuggly	Hercules
Cutiepie	Midnight Ninja
Hiccup	The Admiral
Puddles	Giant Killer
Scooter	Silver Bullet
Splat	The Bone Collector

Billy

Now THOSE are REAL dogs names! -Billy

Does anyone else smell that? -DD

Oh man! I think Mr. Snuffles did a giant killer splat that hits you like a silver bullet! -Brain

What We Learned This Month.

I have learned that there are 5 types of booger. -Billy

1. THE SNAIL. This booger dribbles out your nose leaving a lovely shiny trail.
2. THE WAVE. This booger is very dry and flat. It likes to flap in and out of your nose when you breath, like its waving hello.
3. THE BURNT COOKIE. This booger is crispy on the outside but soft on the inside.
4. THE JELLO. This booger is very soft, very wet, and very disgusting.
5. THE SNOT ROCKET. This booger is blown at high speeds out of one nostril by putting your finger against the other nostril and blowing hard.

I know there are five types of booger because the D.I.E. Sisters have wiped all of them on me in the past week! I liked them better when they were ignoring me! - Billy

I is learn my girlfriend is the sweetest girl in the holes of the worlds! -Mouse

She told you to say that, didn't she? - Brain

Yes....but she is givings to me 10 cans of soda every days! If I no do's what she say she is stopping. ME NEEDS SODA! - Mouse

Your girlfriend made holes in the world? How big is she? - Rock

I really have to invent a machine that lets me go back in time so I can avoid meeting you two for the first time. - Brain

SODA! - Mouse

Stuff We Didn't Get Grounded For....

- I may have just mailed Mouse's girlfriend a picture of him kissing her best friend.- Billy

- WHAT!? NO! I IS NEVER KISSING HER BEST FRIEND. SHE LOOKS LIKE GOATS! THIS IS BEING TERRIBLES. NOW SHE IS NO GIVINGS ME SODA! - Mouse

- That's why I had to do it Mouse. Last night I used the computer to make a fake picture of you kissing her best friend. It's for your own good! You've been acting crazy lately. I never thought I'd say this but there is such a thing as too much soda! - Billy

- NNNNOOOOOOOOO!!!!!! SSSSOOOODDDDDAAAAA!!!!!!!!!! - Mouse

- Wait....So Mouse kissed a goat? -Rock

- SSSSOOOODDDDDAAAAA!!!!!!!!!! - Mouse

I know it's a little insensitive at a time like this but, CHICKENBUTT! -Si Fi

260

Final Thoughts by Billy

Well, it's been another tough month. Maybe the toughest of them all.

-We lost our base!

-Mouse is addicted to soda!

-We can't breathe in our new base without going blind!

-D.I.E. are doing more bad things to us, than ever!

-Nelson is still grounded!

-We all smell of cheese!

-I got a years worth of wedgies in one week!

-We all have to look after the world's ugliest puppies.

-But, on the plus side, Lou Lou got grounded so things have been quieter around here. At least it's not all bad!

But, this is not the time to feel down guys. We are going to turn this thing around! This is usually the bit where Lou Lou tells me how so, I'm not sure how we'll turn it around but, we will....I'm sure we will!

Don't give up gang. We'll find out what's going, just hang in there, relax, take a deep breath and...............wait, don't do that!

-Billy

Too late! -DD

Who turned the lights out? -Rock

Assignments for Next Month by Billy

<u>D.I.E. Update-</u> The only update we need to be doing about the D.I.E. Sisters is working out how to stop them putting my underwear up my butt! Why don't we leave them alone this month? If I get one more wedgie I might just split in half.

<u>Free Nelson Update-</u> This is it guys. I want around the clock surveillance, I want world class disguises, I want secret gadgets, I want....I want....I want....I want some new ideas on how to rescue Nelson!

<u>Chickenbutt Update</u> – Now that Chickenbutt smells all nice, there's only one thing to do, never, ever, ever let her have any more puppies. Also, it might help us if we try to forget that she is a girl. Maybe that will work with Lou Lou too.

<u>Drinks and Snacks/Fundraising</u> – Our base may be lousy but, if there's one thing we have, it's money! And if we run out of soda, then one of us just has to start dating Mouse's girlfriend!

<u>Protect the Base-</u> Yeah, I don't think anyone wants to break in here; not unless they can live without breathing.

Grounded Gang Out!

Don'ts you dares! She is mine girlfriend! I calls her my little soda machine! I loves her! - Mouse.

Billy

Si Fi

Drool

Lou Lou

Gutsy

DD

Mouse

(Chickenbutt)

Extra Bit....One Week Later...THE PUPPIES!...by Billy

I can't take it anymore! My puppy is driving me crazy! It poops in my bed. It poops in my shoes. It poops in my schoolbag. It's not a puppy, it's a monster! Thankfully, it's nearly over. That's what I wanted to tell you all. Lou Lou's uncle will be here tomorrow to pick them up. Make sure you're here at noon. Oh, and if you want to change their name again, be sure to write it on the list.

Old Names	Puppies New Names	Final Puppy Name
Mr. Snuffles	The Terminator	Leaks Poop
Wrinkly Bear	Vampire Hunter	Homework Eater
Snuggly	Hercules	All Night Barker
Cutiepie	Midnight Ninja	Butt Sniffer
Hiccup	The Admiral	Never Sleeps
Puddles	Giant Killer	Thinks He's a Rat.
Scooter	Silver Bullet	Fart Machine.
Splat	The Bone Collector	A Beautiful Soul, who is help me a lot while I is gives up soda forever....

Bye bye pupeyes. I is loves you's forevers. - Mouse

Dude, someone get him some soda! -DD

I was just given this. -Billy

FOR SALE!
THE GROUNDED GANG BASE
Price: 1 human sacrifice <u>OR</u>
The GG heads on sticks <u>OR</u>
You all act as our dates for the school dance next week.
Lots of Love, but mostly hate,
Danni, Isabelle, Emily

Did they pay you a dollar for this? -Brain

I don't know. They shoved a handful of stuff in my coat pocket. I think they were dollars. -Billy

I'll check for you. -Brain

Nope, its boogers. -Brain

I sold another one! And this one didn't pay in boogers! -Billy

FOR SALE....SOCK PUPPETS ....ONLY $5 each

Put them on your hands and entertain your friends!
Can also be used as.... just socks!
Put them on your feet to keep them warm! One price, twice the fun!
Coming soon: Glove puppets! Can also be used as ...just gloves!

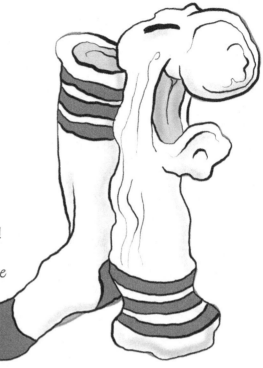

APRIL

P.S. Don't just take your socks off and make your own puppets! This was my idea so no stealing! See locker 217 for details.

April Meeting by Lou Lou

A letter not from The President:

Well, it had to happen one day. Billy's grounded! So, he gave me the book and said I should be President this month.

I know it may be confusing for you all to have a President who makes sense and talks about important things but, don't worry. One day there will be a woman President in charge of the whole country and you'll be able to enjoy it all the time! It might even be me!

So, let's get down to business. First thing you will see is that we are back in our own base! I made a deal with the D.I.E. Sisters! As President I shall leave a space below, for you all to write how great I am.

> In my country there is woman President. She is also horse. We is having a female horse for a President. She is called nightMARE! -Mouse

> Now I is no addicted to soda I is learning how jokes is working. Si Fi is helpings me. -Mouse

> Is funny, no? -Mouse

NO! -Lou Lou

HEY, WAIT A MINUTE! -Brain

Did you tell them we'd go to the dance with them? -Brain

What? -Si Fi

Chickenbutt....and yes, I did say that you were all willing to go to the dance with them. -Lou Lou

Why? -Brain

Why? -Gutsy

Why? -DD

Why's? -Mouse

Why? -Si Fi

Why? -Rock

Why? -Drool

Two reasons....
1. I am not going to spend one more second in that disgusting base of theirs.
2. Because of this....
-Lou Lou

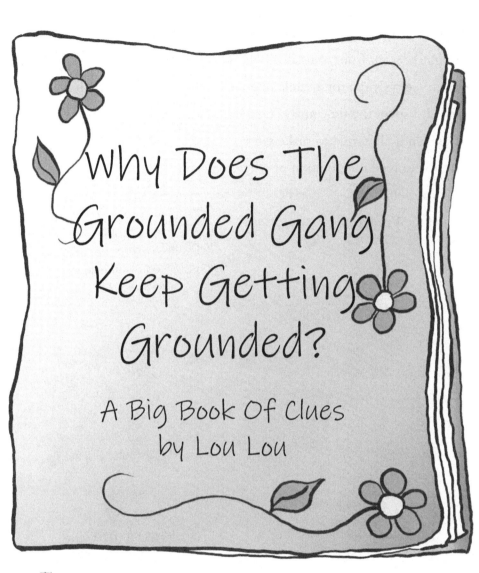

Why Does The Grounded Gang Keep Getting Grounded?

A Big Book Of Clues by Lou Lou

This isn't just lots of girly stuff, is it? -DD

No, but it's lots of stuff by a girl so it's better than anything you've done! - Lou Lou

Girls are mean! -DD

That's right! I've been collecting evidence all along. You see, the clues have been right here, in front of us all along, in this book!

I've been seeing them for a while now and then last month, when I was grounded, I spent the time analyzing everything.

That's when it all started to make sense.

I think I've solved the question of why we keep getting in trouble!

See for yourself.

Then tell me I'm wrong!

I didn't understand any of that. Maybe she's an alien. Hang on, I'll check. -Si Fi

Are you an alien? -Si Fi

No, you big dummy! -Lou Lou

Okay, she checks out. She's good. -Si Fi

You is wrong. -Mouse

Read it first, Mouse!....Why am I in this gang again? -Lou Lou

The Clues....by Lou Lou

Clue #1- The Necklaces.

Have you noticed that our enemies all wear the same necklace? Have you also noticed that it's the same one as the all the cats wear?

Clue # 2 – The Cats.

They are always around the enemies! Look at the photos Billy took. There are cats in all of them!

Clue #3 - The Lists.

Remember the list that Mouse pulled out of the trash can he peed in? It had our names listed on it. The list was in exactly the same order as the list that was written on the wall in D.I.E.'s base!

Clue #4 - The Noise.

That orange tent that keeps moving down our street? It only ever stops outside of the house of someone who is grounded!

Clue # 5 – The Neighbors.

When the enemies moved into our neighborhood, they surrounded us. But they only moved into the houses with no kids living in them!

Clue #6– The Tools.

When the enemies went to Nelson's house, they were all carrying tools, tools that are used for digging!

Clue # 7- Nelson.

When Nelson went missing, he was just about to tell you something big. I think he found out what was going on, so someone had him grounded…to shut him up!

Clue # 8- The Map.

I made a list of the order we were all grounded. Then I made a map of where we all live. Do you see it? We were grounded whenever they needed to dig outside our house so we couldn't disturb them! That's why that annoying orange tent was always outside. They were out there working!

September   Si Fi and Mouse
October   DD and Rock
November   Gutsy
December   Drool
January   Mouse
February   Brain
March   Lou Lou

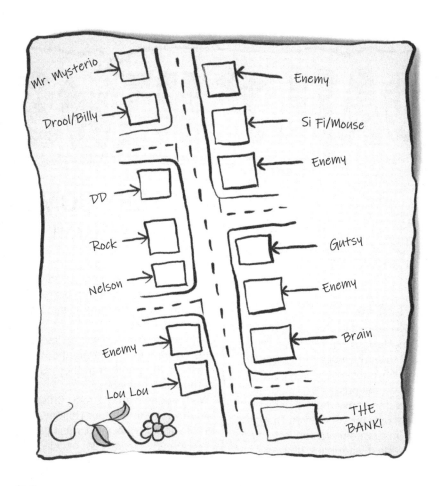

Clue # 9-

I did a little research on Nelson's 'neighbor' and look what I found!

DAILY NEWS

MYSTERY COMES TO TOWN!

The mysterious Mr. Mysterio moved to our town this week bringing with him his hypnosis services....and a controversial past.

Mr. Mysterio says that he uses his talents only for good, even though many in town already feel otherwise. "He made my cat think he was a dog!" said Mildred Brown, 73. "He kept barking and chasing cars!" Meanwhile, Mr. Mysterio says he is only here to help.

"I seek only to help adults and animals with my hypnosis. Sadly, I cannot hypnotize children or I would help them too. But, people should not fear my gift."

Local police say they will be keeping a close eye on Mr. Mysterio and want to reassure the public that there is nothing to worry about.

"We think he's great!" said Officer Smith. "He came to our Holiday Party and hypnotized us all. It was hilarious! He even gave us all cool necklaces!" Time will tell if Mr. Mysterio is here for the right reasons. But, having met him, I can only say that he is the most wonderful man in the world.

Hey! He was there the day my robot went crazy! -Brain

And when we stole Nelsons file! -Rock

And when I broke Needles window! -Drool

The Clues....What They All Mean! ....by Lou Lou

Do you see now? Isn't it obvious?

Is it aliens? -Si Fi

Someone else has been getting us in trouble all along!

I knew it! It's Santa, isn't it? He's mad at me! -Rock

Someone, who uses transmitters hidden inside necklaces to give orders?

Is goat! Is always goat! -Mouse

Someone, who can control animals and adults but not children!

Substitute teachers? -Gutsy

Someone, who makes our enemies do things to us so we get grounded! Like activating a killer robot in a school locker, or stealing files from the file room?

Or making me get bad marks on tests? No wait, that's on me. -Rock

Someone, who had to keep getting us grounded so we wouldn't notice what they were up to!

Someone, who has a plan called Operation Goldenmind!

Someone, who is using mind control, and an army of cats to build a tunnel, right into the bank vault!

Someone called....Mr. Mysterio!

Oh, that's clever! I never saw that coming! - Si Fi

Me either! -Drool

I knew it all along, I just didn't want to show off. -Rock

Now a big space for you to tell me how great I am! ....Lou Lou

Okay, nice theory, but if all of this is true why wasn't Rock attacked by the cat that he took the collar from? -Brain

Don't you remember? He was wearing headphones! His music was blocking Mr. Mysterio's transmitter! -Lou Lou

HEADPHONES! Is that why there were voices in my head? - Rock

Okay, first of all Rock....REALLY!? And secondly, Lou Lou, that's all fine but, you still haven't explained why you want us to go to the dance with the D.I.E. Sisters. Shouldn't we be calling the police instead? -Brain

You want to go to the dance with the police now? And I'm the stupid one! -Rock

Don't you think I tried going to the police? I went to the station but, look.... -Lou Lou

Lou Lou Goes to The Police Station....by Lou Lou

See what I mean? Mysterio has hypnotized the police too!
-Lou Lou

Okay, so we can't go to the police. I still don't see why we have to go to the dance with the D.I.E. Sisters! I mean, I like having our base back....but, it's the D.I.E. Sisters! -Brain

Don't you see? If we're going to stop them, we have to know when they're planning on breaking into the bank. Them asking you to the dance can only mean one thing....it's going to be that night! The whole town will be there so, it will be easy for Mr. Mysterio to do what he wants! It's a perfect plan! That's why I said you'd go to the dance with the D.I.E. Sisters, so we can stop him! -Lou Lou

It sounds dangerous. -Drool

Yeah, I don't think I want to do that. -DD

Me neither, I think I'll give it a miss. -Si Fi

Yeah, it sounds like a lot of work. -Gutsy

But, here's the thing,.....I think he's planning on blaming the bank robbery on Billy! That's why the D.I.E. Sisters weren't allowed to get rid of him. Their boss needs him! Think about it,.....he's the only one in town who won't be at the party and if they follow the tunnel out of the bank, it goes right to Billy's house! All they have to do is destroy the bit of tunnel between Mysterio's house and Billy's and he'll get all the blame! -Lou Lou

It still sounds dangerous! -Drool

Yeah, I still think I don't want to do it? -DD

Yeah, I still think I'll still give it a miss. -Si Fi

Yeah, it still sounds like a lot of work. — Gutsy

But he's your leader! You can't just leave him....it's wrong! -Lou Lou

It still sounds dangerous though! -Drool

Yeah, I'm really pretty sure I don't want to do it. -DD

Yeah, I'm sure I'll give it a miss! -Si Fi

Yeah, it definitely still sounds like a lot of work! - Gutsy

Have you thought that you'll be heroes if you do this? Everyone will love you all again! And have you forgotten that all your money is in that bank? Billy's the only one with the account number. No Billy means no money, which means no candy or soda! -Lou Lou

Right! We have to do something! -Drool

Absolutely! This cannot be allowed to happen! -DD

We have to put a stop to this! -Si Fi

Let's get to work on a plan already! -Gutsy

The Plan.... Give me your ideas....by Lou Lou

What if we called the interplanetary police and said we needed help? -Si Fi

~~HELP~~

Hey, what if we is calling my Uncle Miroslava? His job is stopping crime. He can help us? On no, waits. His job is to do crimes. He is criminal. Yeah, I think he no help us. -Mouse

What if I was to dress as a cat and try to infiltrate Mysterio's base? All I need is two weeks and the ability to shrink and grow fur. -DD

What if we just let Mr. Mysterio blame Billy. I think I can survive with no soda if I don't have to have a big brother. -Drool

What if we took Mysterio out to dinner and then persuaded him it was all one big mistake? We could get Chinese food. No wait, let's get Indian! Or Mexican? Maybe Italian?....I'm so hungry now....wait, what were we talking about again? -Gutsy

What if we go to the bank and tell them we'll take all of the money and look after it for a few weeks? -Rock

Don't you have to be stupid somewhere else?
-Brain

Not for a couple of hours. -Rock

The Real Plan....by Lou Lou

Well, now that you have no doubt wasted a whole page with your stupid ideas, here's the real plan!

We form three teams; Team A, Team B, and Team C.

Team A will go to the dance with the D.I.E. Sisters.

Team B will sneak into the tunnel and stop the robbery.

Team C will stay at a safe distance and write down what's happening to the other teams.

I, for one, is being on Team C please and thank-you's! -Mouse

Me too. -Gutsy

Me three! Team C for me! -Drool

Me five. In case you need someone good at math and stuff. -Rock

Sorry boys....the teams are as follows..... -Lou Lou

Team A	Team B	Team C
Rock	DD	Lou Lou
Brain	Mouse	
	Si Fi	
	Gutsy	
	Drool	

Oh, come on! -Brain

The plan is to stop the bank raid and get evidence that Mr. Mysterio is behind all of this. To do this, some of us (Team A), will make him think we are at the dance, where he wants us. Then, when he isn't thinking about us anymore, some of us (Team B), will go down the tunnel to stop the raid on the bank. While all of this is going on, some of us (Team C), will keep a record of everything that is happening,….for evidence,….just in case something goes wrong and we need proof that we were only trying to help. Your missions are attached. Take them, learn them by heart, then destroy them. We'll all meet at our base the night of the dance.

How about some of us (Team C), stop giving all the dangerous jobs to other people? - Gutsy

If you stop complaining you can destroy your mission by eating it. -Lou Lou

Already did….can I eat everyone elses? -Gutsy

Alright! After you've all learned your missions by heart, please give them to Gutsy to eat. -Lou Lou

Some of us, (Team C), are the best! -Gutsy

Your Mission: Team A

Brain and Rock

Brain, I need you to make five fake Grounded Gang members out of that polymere solution you invented. Then, I need you to put them all in costumes and sit them in the corner, at the dance, so it looks like we're all there. Then all you both have to do is keep the D.I.E. Sisters distracted and Team B will be free to do their part of the plan. Oh, and can you put a microphone and a camera in one of the dummies heads so I can record everything that happens? Thanks! You're the best!

So, you want me to make 5 dummies but then you give me the biggest dummy as a partner? -Brain

That's not very nice. Who are you talking about? -Rock

You! -Brain

Oh, that's okay then.... Hey, wait a minute! -Rock

Your Mission: Team B

DD, Mouse, Si Fi, Gutsy, and Drool

With the D.I.E. Sisters thinking you five are all at the dance, you'll be free to sneak down the tunnel, go into the bank, and catch Mysterio in the act! Take lots of pictures! He can't be controlling all the police and we need to have proof that this is all Mysterio's plan….and that Billy is innocent!

There's a list of equipment you need to bring below;
Flashlights
Gutsy's sisters camera phone,……so you can send me pictures straight away.
1 Walkie Talkie,……..so you can tell me what's happening.
1 Music player with headphones

Other stuff we need to bring! -Team B

    Weapons!

      Anti-stupid pills ⎯⎯⎯⎯⎯⎯▶ Are these real? -Rock

    More weapons!

    Candy

      Extra weapons

    Soda

      Rain coats ⎯⎯⎯⎯⎯⎯▶ We'll be in a tunnel! -Gutsy

Your Mission: Team C

Lou Lou

I will record everything that is happening, in a book, that I made especially.

Please tell me it doesn't have flowers on the cover? -DD

It has flowers on the cover. -Lou Lou

More **April** One week later

Operation Stop Operation Goldenmind

Also known as 'what happens when your plan goes wrong! -Si Fi

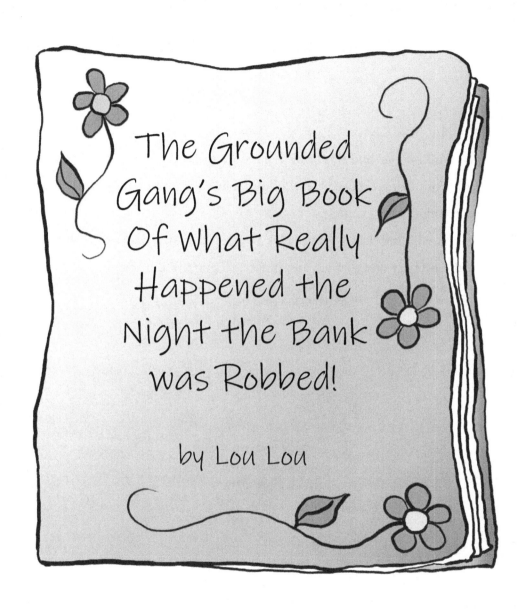

The Story of What Really Happened the Night the Bank was Robbed

by The Grounded Gang

HER gang?! -DD

To Whom it May Concern,

My name is Lou Lou and this book is a record of how my gang tried to stop the bank from being robbed. Here follows a live account of all our communications that evening.

I think you will find that it proves that NO-ONE in my gang was a willing part of the robbery and that we are, in fact, all good kids just trying to do the right thing.

And if you're thinking of giving out a reward we only accept cash....we're good, not stupid! -Si Fi

We would also like immunity from anything bad we might do in the future. Not that we have anything planned....you know, just in case! -Drool

The Night of the Dance.

A record of everything we said....by Lou Lou

8pm

Lou Lou – "Team A? This is Team C. Are you in position?"

Team A- "This is Brain. We are in position….just! Gutsy's head fell off, twice, on the way here and Drool's leg was stolen by a dog but, all five of our dummies are in position and ready. Sending you a picture from the Mousecam now….just so you know, that's what I call the camera I put in the fake Mouse's head. Cool name right!

Lou Lou – "Err, Brain? What happened to the polymere dummies you were supposed to make?"

Team A – "Hey! You try making five life size dummies in a week! This was as good as I could do!"

Lou Lou – "Okay!....Can you see the D.I.E. Sisters? Do they think that the dummies are real?"

Team A – "I can see them. They are watching us from across the room and, they seem to be buying it so far. I'm not sure what they'll think if they come closer though? Just in case, Rock is ready to intercept them with what he calls his 'sweet dance moves'. I'm hoping they'll think he has something medically wrong with him and back off."

Lou Lou – "Thank-you Team A. I'll tell Team B they are a go."

Lou Lou – "Team B, this is Lou Lou. Are you in position?"

Team B – "Lou Lou, this is being Mouse. Team B is talking and we is deciding we is wanting to have news name. We is no like Team B. We is preferring Team Dark Wolfs Blood Ninjas."

Lou Lou – "Negative, Team B. We don't have time to change team names."

Team B – "Lou Lou? This is Gutsy. We are really going to need you to call us Team Dark Wolfs Blood Ninjas if you want us to carry on."

Lou Lou – "Negative, Team B. We don't have time for this!"

Team B – "Lou Lou, this is DD. The new name is kind of a deal breaker for us!"

Lou Lou – "This is so stupid! Okay,…Team Dark Wolfs Blood Ninjas,….are you in position?"

Team Dark Wolfs Blood Ninjas – "Team Dark Wolfs Blood Ninjas are in position."

Lou Lou – "Do you have all of your equipment?"

Team Dark Wolfs Blood Ninjas – "Team Dark Wolfs Blood Ninjas have everything."

Lou Lou – "Are you sure?"

Team Dark Wolfs Blood Ninjas – "Team Dark Wolfs Blood Ninjas are sure!"

Team A – "Lou Lou. This is Rock. We've been talking and we've decided we'd like a new name too. We'd like to be called Team Lou Lou Fart Face."

Lou Lou – "RIGHT! BOTH TEAMS, THAT'S ENOUGH! YOU ARE GOING TO BE CALLED TEAMS A AND B! UNDERSTAND?"

(2 minutes of silence.)

Team A – "We understand. Sorry."

Team B – "Sorry."

Lou Lou – "Right! Let's proceed. Team B. Send me a picture of your location."

Lou Lou – "Negative on the picture, Team B. It just came out blank. Can you try and send me a picture, of your location, again?"

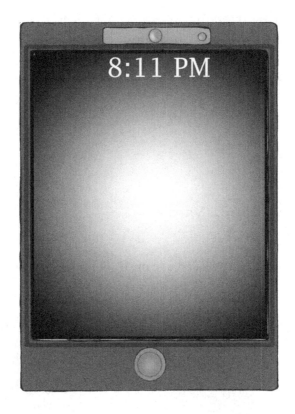

Lou Lou - "Same problem again, Team B. It's still too dark. Can you turn up the flashlight?"

Team B – "Afraid we can't do that! SOMEONE forgot the flashlights!"

Team B – "This is Si Fi. I didn't forget them....I just forgot the batteries."

Lou Lou – "WHAT!? How are you going to see where you're going?"

Team B – "Lou Lou. This is being Mouse. Is okay. I is very good at seeings in the dark. I can be leading us all the....OWWW!...I is bangings my heads....OWWW! My foot!"

Lou Lou – "Oh, good grief. Just go slowly Team B. And be careful!"

8:20 PM

Lou Lou – "Team A. Are the D.I.E. Sisters still convinced that our gang is all at the dance?"

Team A – "Thats a yes. They are still watching us and they seem to be convinced."

Lou Lou – "Great news, Team A. Team B, how are you doing?"

Team B – "HELP! This is Team B! We need help! It's awful!"

Lou Lou – "TEAM B, TEAM B, IS EVERYTHING OKAY?"

Team B – "Oh the humanity! Why……WHY?"

Lou Lou – "TEAM B, WHAT'S HAPPENING? DO YOU NEED HELP?"

Team B – "*(cough)* Lou Lou, *(cough)* tell my family *(cough)* I love them!"

Lou Lou – "Oh no. This is awful! They're dying!"

Team B – "Lou Lou, this is Gutsy. That's a negative on the emergency. I just farted and they are all being a little bit dramatic!"

Team B – "Lou Lou, this is being Mouse. We is no ables to breath. I thinks my hairs is falling outs…."

Lou Lou – "BOYS! PULL YOURSELVES TOGETHER…NOW! Right, let's try this again. Team B, what is your position?"

Team B – "This is DD. We are most of the way down the tunnel. We can see a light in the distance. Wait, I hear something….Oh no! It's meowing! There are cats up there!"

Lou Lou – "Quickly, Team B, turn on the headphones. You have to block the radio signal to the cats."

Team B – "Will do Lou Lou. Turning on headphones now"…. *(go round and round, round and round, round and round.)*

Lou Lou – "Team B….Is that 'wheels on the bus' I can hear playing?"

Team B – (*The babies on the bus go whah whah whah, whah whah whah!)*

Lou Lou – "How old are you boys?"

Team B – "This is Si Fi. Sorry about that, it's my little sisters music player."

Team B – "This is being Mouse and Si Fi is no havings a little sisters."

Team B – "Give….me….that….this is Si Fi. I think we had some technical difficulties there. Music is now turned down. The meowing has stopped."

Lou Lou – "Thank you, Team B. Proceed toward the light and tell me what you see, when you get there."

8:30 PM

Team B – "We are at the end of tunnel, Lou Lou. The music player seems to be working. The cats are just sitting around, ignoring us. We are proceeding into the bank now."

Lou Lou – "Okay Team B. Whatever you do, do be careful."

Team B – "Ha ha! You said do-do!"

8:31PM

Team A – "Lou Lou! I think we may have a problem. Now Mouses ex-girlfriend is here, and she looks mad! She's heading this way. Rock's on his way to stop her with his dance moves."

Lou Lou – "Keep me updated Team A."

Team A – "That's a negative on Rock slowing her down. She kicked him in the leg and he is now hopping around the dance floor. A group has formed around him. They think he is dancing. They obviously haven't noticed that he's crying. Oh no! She's trying to talk to Mouse. I'm on my way to stop her!"

Lou Lou – "Be careful Brain!"

(5 seconds later)

Team A – "In….pain….It burns….She has a….kick like….a donkey!"

Lou Lou- "Brain, were you able to stop her?"

Team A – "Negative….Lou Lou….she kicked me….in the ….can't walk….ever again….she's talking to the fake Mouse now!"

Team B- "Lou Lou. We are inside the bank! We can see all the enemies loading bags of money into a wagon."

Lou Lou- "Stay where you are Team B. Team A is in trouble. It may be dangerous for you to go ahead."

Team B- "Did you just say you want us to go to bed?"

Lou Lou – "Negative Team B, I said do not go ahead."

Team B – "Errr….thanks Lou Lou, but we're not sleepy…. I think we may be having trouble with this walkie-talkie. You're breaking up Lou Lou…."

Team B – "Don't worry. We're moving in to get a picture."

Team A – "Lou Lou, this is Brain. Mouse's ex-girlfriend is getting mad that he won't talk to her….oh no! She's offering him soda!"

Team B – "We're nearly there, Lou Lou!"

Team A – "OH NO! She just poured soda into Mouse's mouth. He's starting to short circuit……..smoke coming out of his ears……….sparks coming out of his mouth………"

Lou Lou – "Team A! Team B! ABORT! ABORT! All of you, get out of there, the plan failed!"

Team A – "Lou Lou, Mouse's head just exploded! The D.I.E. Sisters are onto us! They are making a phone call now!"

Team B – "Lou Lou, we are nearly in position….wait, one of the enemies phones is ringing….it's The Hammer….he's talking….he just shouted 'WHAT!' into the phone….oh no, someone just shouted 'CHICKENBUTT' back at him!"

Lou Lou – "Team B! Run, NOW!"

Team B – "They are onto us….they're coming this way….we're running….oh no, the meowing has started again….trying to turn on music….oh no….batteries are dead….music not working! Cats are getting louder!...Enemies are behind us!...Nowhere to run!...We're trapped!"

Lou Lou – "Team B? Are you okay?"

Team B – "Batteries dying on walking-talkie….it's too late….they are going to………"

END OF TRANSMISSION….

THE END....

....of ~~April~~ was really bad so, why don't we move onto May?

I didn't sell this one....it sells itself! -Billy

Feeling low? Wishing you could be a better person? Why not spend time with a real hero!? Learn the secrets of my bravery and stop being the loser you are! (When you compare yourself to me!)
Only $5 for 30 minutes of my precious time.*
*Photos are extra.

The Billy!

MAY

Ummmmm guys....? -Drool

May Meeting....by Billy

Letter from The President,

Well, it's good to be back! And I know you're all happy to have me return....you know, after I saved you last month! Well, let me just say that you are very welcome and then we'll say no more about it....what's that? I'm being too humble and you think I should at least write about what happened so it can be recorded forever in the Grounded Gang's book? You think that even though everyone in town knows I'm a hero you still feel that it's important for me to record our gang's proudest moments? Well, who am I to deny the story from the future generations of grounded kids?....I mean, they'll probably want to name their kids after me when they hear it but hey, if that's what you want, who am I to stop you! Oh, and I hear rumors that you are planning a surprise party to give me an award for being the bravest member of The Grounded Gang....ever? Well, I just wanted to say that, there's really no need....but try to avoid Tuesday. The local newspaper wants to interview me that day.

-Billy

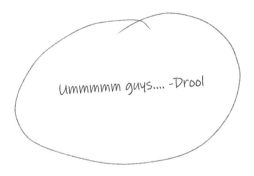

Ummmmm guys..... -Drool

(Guys!? -Drool)

Billys Guide to How to be a Hero by Billy

Or how I almost, singlehandedly, stopped Operation Goldenmind AND saved the gang, the bank, the town, the world.

So, where were we? Oh yes, that's right. Mouse's head had just exploded and the D.I.E. Sisters had discovered that DD, Si Fi, Gutsy and Drool weren't really at the dance, after all. So, they called the enemies who had surrounded the gang and were just about to take them prisoner. Lou Lou's plan had failed, all hope was gone.

But, they had forgotten about one thing…me….Billy!

That's right. For just as The Grounded Gang thought they were finished, Billy burst out the tunnel!

Jumping in front of Mr. Mysterio, he threw a handful of new batteries at his gang and ordered them to put on the music, neutralizing the threat from the cats. Then, with a wave of his hand, he ordered the gang to run down the tunnel, away from the enemies, while he stayed and provided cover for his friends. All around him, doors began to crash and sirens began to scream. But Billy remained unmoving, strong, refusing to let the enemies pass, until every last member of his gang was safe!

Operation Goldenmind had failed. The enemies had been stopped. Billy had saved the day. He was….a hero!

You see guys, that's how it happened. Some of us are just born for greatness….and others….well, they just aren't me is all.

GUYS!?
-Drool

Drool, that's enough! Can't you see that everyone just wants to read how great I am? -Billy

Well, I just thought that everyone might like to see this! -Drool

Hey! That's my diary!....You're not allowed to touch that! -Billy

I know....but we'd run out of toilet paper.... -Drool

You are in so much trouble! -Billy

Dear Diary   April 27th

So, a lot of good things have happened lately!
- We stopped Mr. Mysterio from robbing the bank!
- The D.I.E. Sisters are leaving us alone....so far!
- The Enemies have returned to being normal....well, as normal as they can be, for anyone who has just been hypnotized and doesn't remember anything that happened for the last year!
- The bank manager gave me a bunch of money as a thank-you for saving the bank!
- Best of all, none of us has been grounded for 2 weeks!

But do you know what's even better than all of that? I'm a hero! Everyone thinks I'm the one who stopped Operation Goldenmind!

But I want to confess something to you, diary....it's not true! You see, that night, I wasn't really trying to save everyone. In fact, I was only in the tunnel by accident! You see, I was grounded but, I was desperate for new ideas on how to stop the enemies. So, that night, when I looked out my window and saw the orange tent outside my house, I decided to explore.

I put on my bunny slippers, grabbed my camera, snuck outside, and slipped into the tent.

And guess what? This time there were no cats! Then I saw it....the hole! Okay, I didn't really see the hole....it was dark and I was sleepy, so I fell into the hole....but that's kind of like finding it, if you forget all of my injuries! Anyway, so now I was stuck in a dark tunnel, not knowing how to get out!

That's when I heard it, my favorite song, wheels on the bus! Now I know that I'm a little old for it, and I could only ever admit this to you diary, but I just can't help loving that song! It's just too catchy!

So, I followed the sound thinking that nothing bad could possibly happen in a place that played wheels on the bus! But, when I got to the end of the tunnel, the music suddenly stopped. That's when I saw the gang hiding up ahead. I was about to hide myself when I heard a phone ringing.

Then someone shouted, "WHAT!" so I shouted, "CHICKENBUTT!"

I didn't mean to, it just came out of my mouth before I knew what was happening. But, by then, it was too late. That's when I saw who the gang were hiding from....the enemies!

Suddenly, there was meowing all around the gang and I realized they were surrounded by cats! Before they could even try to escape, the enemies were surrounding them too....they were trapped!

I knew I had to do something, but what? Should I jump in and destroy them with my karate? Should I strike fear into them with my judo skills? No, there was only one thing to do....run away and save myself! And that's what I was about to do, when I felt a hand on my shoulder. It was Lou Lou. She was all out of breath and talking too fast about some back-up plan! I don't really remember it all, to be honest. I was just waiting for her to stop talking so I could run away. But I do remember it was something to do with her having another plan, in case ours didn't work?

In that plan, she had to get the bank manager to bring the police to the bank. So, she needed to make something crazy happen at the dance; something so crazy that everyone would believe her when she told them that the bank was being robbed,....something as crazy as the bank manager watching Mouse's head land in the punch bowl just before he got a phone call telling him to get to the bank very, very quickly!

And, all of this had happened because she called Mouse's ex-girlfriend and told her that he'd date her again....if she just went to the dance and gave him some soda!

I don't know. It was something like that. The bit I do remember is the part where she said we needed to save the gang, from the enemies, until the bank manager got there with the police. I remember that bit, clearly, because it really made me want to run away!

To make things worse, while she'd been talking, Mr. Mysterio had shown up. He was so mad! Maybe it was because his plan was in trouble, or maybe it was because he shouted, "WHAT!", when he saw the gang were all there and someone shouted, "CHICKENBUTT," back? Alright, it was me again, but it's not my fault. It's the law! Anyway, Mr. Mysterio went over and grabbed DD, thinking it was him who had shouted it. This is when Lou Lou whispered in my ear that we had to help him, which I wanted to do,.....I just wanted to run away more. So, that's what I did. But, as I started to run, Lou Lou instead pushed me the other way and I tripped, right into the back of Mr. Mysterio!

So, I was sitting on top of Mr. Mysterio, who'd let go of DD, while the gang was looking at me all confused. And that's when everything went really crazy! Lights started flashing, horns started blaring, and over my shoulder I saw Lou Lou, in the shadows, throw a bunch of batteries to the gang. Next thing I knew they were all escaping down the tunnel, while the cats and enemies stood around, looking very confused! Then, more lights started flashing and I could see people standing in the bank vault. I didn't know what to do. So, I climbed off Mr. Mysterio and he jumped up, shouting something about swearing revenge on our gang, before running away.

Next thing I knew someone was standing over me, the bank manager. He pointed at me and started telling me how he saw me tackle the man who was robbing the bank and how I'd saved the day!

Meanwhile, all of the enemies were sitting around like they had no clue how they got there. It was only when I explained to the bank manager that Mr. Mysterio was the one I'd ~~been pushed into~~ tackled, like a ninja, that he realized that they must have been hypnotized and weren't to blame.

Of course, it might have been good if I'd told him that straight away. To be honest, I was still in shock that Lou Lou had put me in such incredible danger that I couldn't speak. Thankfully, they eventually decided to follow the tunnel....which led them to Mr. Mysterio's house. He was long gone by then, but never mind, I was still a hero!

And that's the truth dear diary. It was Lou Lou and not me who saved the day.

Of course, I did go and talk to her. I said I'd tell everyone the truth but she said not to bother. She was so happy that she wasn't going to be in trouble anymore that she didn't even want any of the reward money! And, she'd prefer it if I took all the credit! Then, she called the newspaper and told them that it was me who'd called the bank manager that night! Now, the whole town ~~knows~~ thinks I'm a hero!

Now diary, I know its not really fair for me to do it but, I have decided to do what she asked. I do feel guilty about it....a little guilty....but I'm willing to be a hero if that's what she wants. I won't make a big deal about it. I probably won't even mention it.

Thanks for listening diary....and for keeping my secret. -Billy

May ......One week later.

Another letter from The President, - Billy

Well, obviously, I haven't been around much lately. I know you're mad at me, and I get it! You read my diary and you're angry that I didn't tell you it was Lou Lou, not me, who saved the day. So, I've been staying away, especially as everyone in town still thinks that it was me who saved the bank,....but come on, they think you're all great too....okay, that's not true....but, they don't think you're bad anymore!

Anyway, after talking with Brain this week, I decided it was time for me to come back. I know you all decided that there was something that I had to do first, but even so I appreciate you letting me remain as your leader...and for not telling everyone, in town, the truth.

I understand that I have to pay the price for lying to you all about who saved you. So, as agreed, here goes....

> I, Billy, aged 13, would like everyone to know that I would like to marry a monkey and live with it forever and ever in our little monkey house. I will then spend my days making it banana pies and cleaning its armpits with my toothbrush which I like to keep in the toilet. I also like to collect farts in jars, eat other people's boogers, and one day hope to marry the tooth fairy. Oh, I also wear bunny slippers and my favorite song is 'Wheels on the bus.' I would like this letter to be shown to everyone at school, even if I say I don't, because it's all true. Oh.....and I've never changed my underwear....ever!
> -Billy

A Page for You All To Tell Me What You Think? -Billy

I still don't know if we should forgive him. -Si Fi

I don't know either....I mean he did lie to us. -Gutsy

Yeah, we're like family! And you don't lie to family! -DD

You can share the reward money if you forgive me. - Billy

How much is they giving you. -Mouse

$500 -Billy

Forgiven! -Mouse

Forgiven! -Si Fi

Forgiven! -Brain

Forgiven! -DD

Forgiven! -Gutsy

Forgiven! -Rock

Forgiven! -Drool

Grounded Gang Central

Stuff for May

Roll call

Secret smell of the month

Password for the month

New clubhouse rules

Free Nelson update

D.I.E. update

What we learned this month

Stuff we didn't get grounded for this month

Final thoughts

Assignments for next month *No assignments!....It's summertime!*

Rollcall

HERE	GROUNDED

Nelson ✓

Billy ✓

Brain ✓

Double Dare ✓

Mouse ✓

Si Fi ✓

Rock ✓

Gutsy ✓

Lou Lou ✓

Drool ✓

Chickenbutt

(Chickenbutt)

Secret Smell of the Month....by Billy

No secrets, this month, guys. Life is good! We no longer have to live in fear of the enemies now that they are no longer hypnotized. And as for the D.I.E. sisters,....well I don't think we've seen the last of them. But as long as they have to keep a low profile, I think we're safe from wedgies for a while! That is why, this month, the smell is success! We're not getting grounded anymore, we have our base back, we have T.V. video games, a mascot, candy, money, soda. We almost have it all. So, breathe deeply, guys, we did it!

I always thought success would smell sweeter.....then, I found out it was one of Gutsy's old gym socks down the back of the couch. -Brain

Where did you put it? I was saving some cheese in there? -Gutsy

Password for the Month

This months password will be:

Izzy Backyet

Well.....is he? -Brain

New Clubhouse Rules

Okay guys, we have money, and school is about to end for the summer. Three months of freedom is nearly here! So, let's try and think of some things that will really make the base better for our vacation....

	YES	NO
Let's put in a pool, oh, and a hot tub! -DD	✓✓✓✓	✓
We could have a cupboard full of emergency pants....in case anyone forgets theirs! -Rock	✓	????
We should start a lost and found! So, for instance, say I found someone's old tissue stuck to my face after I took a nap on the couch, I could find who 'lost' it....and kill them! -Drool	✓✓✓✓✓	Ha Ha!
We should be livings large. I is wanting my owns private toilet trash can....with a curtain! No, no sorry. I know I ask too much now. I is crazy. For a seconds there I am thinkings that we is millyairs! -Mouse	✓✓	
How about a robot that cooks, cleans, and rubs my feet while I play video games? We can call it 'G.I.R.L.' -Si Fi	✓✓✓✓✓✓	♡

Eeeerr, yeah. I'll get to that in a minute.... -Billy

Hey! I thought we were a boys only gang again? -DD

324

Free Nelson Update

by Billy

Days Grounded: 484

Okay guys, a good as everything is right now, we all know that one thing is still missing from our gang....Nelson! After everything that happened I thought he'd be set free, but when I went to his house and asked his mom if I could see him, she said he was still grounded and would be for a very, very long time. I asked her what he'd done but, she said it was none of my business and maybe I should think about getting a new friend.....in case I never saw Nelson again! Then, she told me to leave. Okay, she told me to leave after I asked her if she could quickly make me some of her famous cookies, but that doesn't change anything. Mr. Mysterio is gone. The enemies are no longer under his control. The cats are all gone. But, Nelson is still grounded.

I don't know what to tell you guys. We need to get back to work. Nelson needs us more than ever. So, I decided to hire someone who's really good at this stuff.

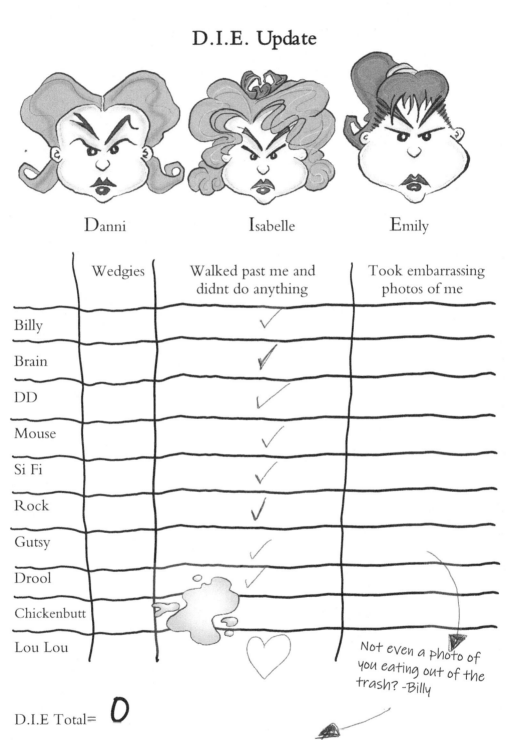

What We Learned This Month

Lou Lou is too clever for you! -Lou Lou

Some fruit is made of wax? How sick is that? -Gutsy

My girlfriend still loves me! I is what you call a chicken magnet! -Mouse

When your friend explodes in a room full of people do not rip him apart to try to save the expensive camera in his head....some people will think that you are trying to murder him! -Brain

I am not the only one who likes wheels on the bus! -Si Fi

Big brothers will pay big bucks to get their diaries back! -Drool

My dance moves get sweeter and sweeter! -Rock

Nelson needs us more than ever! -Billy

Stuff We Didn't Get Grounded For....

I drew a picture on the back of my old glasses and told Si Fi they were alien x-ray glasses. -Gutsy

I put itching powder in my sister's bra! -Drool

I snuck up behind Mouse dressed as a goat. It was hilarious! -DD

I gave my little brother fake money. -Billy

I saw a naked alien in my Mom's bathroom. – Si Fi

I drew fake eyes on my eyelids so I could take a nap in class. -Rock

I is going to kill a goat! -Mouse

You did get in trouble for that though, remember? You drew three eyes! -Brain

Final Thoughts by Billy

Well, guys, it's been a long, hard school year but the Grounded Gang finally did it. We are no longer grounded! And, now that school is about to finish, we are free men! And, even though Nelson is still grounded, I know that we will free him soon. We did a good job guys and I, for one, am proud of us. If we were all together, I would suggest that we have a group hug. But, instead, I'm going to ask everyone to write some words to sum up how they feel about our gang....Billy

and woman....and you're not men! -Lou Lou

The truth is out there! -Si Fi

Some words -Rock

Boys are dumber than I thought! -Lou Lou

Blavornaschnoogle. -Mouse

Don't trust family! -Drool

Booger! -DD

Where's my cheese? -Gutsy

No more assignments with Rock....ever! -Brain

Real nice guys....real nice! -Billy

Assignments for ~~Next Month~~....

THE SUMMER....also known as DO WHATEVER YOU WANT! by Billy

- Play video games! -Drool

- Learns to sleeps and plays video games at same times! -Mouse

- Find my cheese! -Gutsy

- Use some of the gangs money to help me find aliens. -Si Fi

- Invent a cure for all diseases....OR invent a robot that fires soda into your mouth while you sleep/play video games. -Brain

- Play with Brain's robot! -DD

- Remember to wear pants? -Rock

Well I'm afraid that you'll all be a little busy helping me to free Nelson!
-Lou Lou

Boys rule! -Billy

What? -Lou Lou

Chickenbutt! -Billy

GROUNDED GANG OUT!!!!

Gutsy Rock DD Lou Lou Drool (Chickenbutt)

Billy Mouse Si Fi

331

The End....

Chickenbutt!

Made in the USA
Columbia, SC
03 December 2020